THE OPEN UNIVERSITY

An Arts Foundation Course
Units 22 and 23

Nature, Work and Art

Prepared by Stephen Bayley for the Course Team

The Open University Press

Cover:

William Holman Hunt, *The Awakening Conscience*, oil, exhibited 1854 (see pages 54–5). Reproduced by courtesy of the Tate Gallery, London.

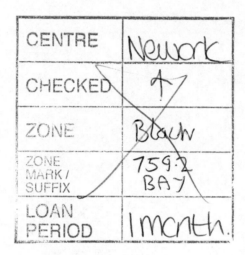
The Open University Press
Walton Hall, Milton Keynes
MK7 6AA

First published 1978. Reprinted 1981 (twice)

Designed by the Graphic Design Group of the Open University.

Printed in Great Britain by
EYRE AND SPOTTISWOODE LIMITED
AT GROSVENOR PRESS PORTSMOUTH

ISBN 0 335 05419 6

This text forms part of an Open University course. The complete list of units in the course appears at the end of this text.

For general availability of supporting material referred to in this text, please write to Open University Educational Enterprises Ltd., 12 Cofferidge Close, Stony Stratford, Milton Keynes, MK11 1BY, Great Britain.

Further information on Open University courses may be obtained from the Admissions Office, The Open University, P.O. Box 48, Walton Hall, Milton Keynes, MK7 6AB.

1.3

CONTENTS

IMPORTANT NOTE

There is a Glossary on pages 73-4 in which some names and terms that occur in these units and that might not be familiar to you are explained.

You will need to consult the Course Reader, *Nature and Industrialization*, Edited by Alasdair Clayre (1977), Oxford University Press/The Open University Press.

The relevant broadcasts are:

Television programme 22, *Turner and Constable*

Television programme 23, *Victorian moral paintings*

Radio programme 22, *The Royal Academy*

Radio programme 23, *Art Distribution*

INTRODUCTION

What happened to art, and in particular, to painting, in the period when industrialization changed Britain from an <u>agrarian</u> to a manufacturing country? In these two units I want to suggest an answer to this question – though you must not expect that answer to be in the form of a catalogue of paintings which naïvely depict the developments that artists observed around them. Certainly some painters, including many of the best known ones, depicted early industry. These pictures show their fascination with, for example, copper mines, ironworks or railways, but were not painted to illustrate any ideological programme.

Figure 1 Paul Sandby, The Iron Forge between Dolgelli and Barmouth in Merionethshire, *aquatint, 1776 (Crown copyright. Reproduced by courtesy of the Trustees of the British Museum: British Museum 1964.8.19.654)*

An argument could, perhaps, be constructed to suggest that every artist of stature was affected and influenced by what industry was doing to the countryside, but I think that any account of art in Britain between 1780 and 1880 which recorded only these scenes of industry and its effect on the natural environment would not only be a very dull work, but would also be historically fraudulent. The changes which did occur in art during this period were, of course, partially generated by the ineluctable presence of 'industrialization', but I feel that the real changes were fundamental ones which ran through the very substructure of art and its place in society – not superficial changes in content and subject matter.

The age of industrialization coincided with the period when art diverged from what had hitherto been an apparently linear development. What happened was not simply that painters such as Paul Sandby (1725–1809) began to paint subjects like copper mines, which had only rarely before been a subject for art (although the novelty of this work *is* a part of the larger issue), but that art appeared now to have a different role in both purpose and stature. In the early part of the period we are studying, it is fair to say that the developments of art in general are directly dependent on developments on landscape painting in particular.

Most people would say that there has always been 'landscape', either in the countryside itself, or as a genre of painting. However, it is important to remember that in historical terms the idea of 'landscape' is relatively new.

Today, when most people live in manufacturing cities which owe their very existence to industrialization, it is hard to imagine that once no pleasure was to be gained from looking at nature – yet this was the case. Indeed, it would be no exaggeration to claim that the landscape, in its sense of being a view which is pleasing to the eye, a sense of beauty in an individual place, was actually *invented* (and I use the word with care) at the beginning of our period.

Figure 2   Vecellio, The Holy Family with Saint John, *oil (Walker Art Gallery, Liverpool)*

The very first use of the word 'landscape' in England has troubled historians for many years. The *Shorter Oxford English Dictionary* lists no usage earlier than 1602, but it was in fact used four years earlier in Richard Haydocke's translation of Lomazzo's *Trattato dell'arte de la pittura* (*Treatise on the Art of Painting*). Haydocke refers to landscape only as a detail which might be used to fill in the backgrounds of a portrait or a religious scene. For instance in Figure 2, *The Holy Family with St John,* the painter has used, as the scene demands, some notation of landscape to establish the setting of his picture. But Vecellio's treatment of the countryside, while charming, lacks any real presence of credence: it is a model landscape, not painted from nature but created out of familiarity with established conventions. Another early use of the word 'landscape' was to describe a straightforward topographical picture, of the sort that might be used by mapmakers or official agents. But the use of the word developed quickly: in *The Art of Drawing with the Pen and Limning in Watercolours* (1606; second edition 1612) the English writer, Henry Peacham, used 'landscape' as a word to describe a proper, though minor, genre of art in its own right.[1]

But there were, nevertheless, few native English painters who practised the art of landscape painting. English buyers who wanted to have landscape pictures hanging on their walls at home had usually to rely on the supply of paintings from Dutchmen resident in England, or on the rather crude pictures of native artists like Robert Streeter (see Figure 3).

Indeed, one of the telling characteristics of the introduction of landscape painting into this country is that although England is rightly regarded as the true home of the genre, the market was supplied first of all by foreigners. Even the Dutch were, to an extent, imitators of the Italians, whose country, in the seventeenth century, provided most landscape painters with their richest source of imagery. Italian scenes, either dreamlike visions of the countryside, or of bandits

[1]Limning is an old word, derived from the word meaning 'illuminate', which used to mean 'painting'. Nicholas Hilliard, the most famous British painter of the seventeenth century, wrote a book called *A Treatise Concerning the Art of Limning*. Hilliard was a friend of Richard Haydocke.

Figure 3   Robert Streeter, Whiteladies and Boscobel House, *oil, c. 1670 (Reproduced by gracious permission of Her Majesty the Queem)*

in dramatic natural surroundings, were *de rigueur* for the painter of landscape. Thus, the single most important influence on the development of a native English school of landscape painting came from a Frenchman resident in Italy, Claude Gellée (also known as Claude Lorraine on account of his birth-place). Claude lived in Italy from about 1613 to his death in 1682. His paintings are always immediately recognizable because they follow a well-tried formula. Sometimes Claude paints a scene from classical myth or history, or, perhaps, a scene from the Bible, but whatever the ostensible subject matter, the real content of any Claude pictures is his own formalized interpretation of scenes observed in the Roman campagna. In the immediate foreground of a Claude picture there is usually a *repoussoir* feature[1], which is dark in colour (often a tree), and which contrasts vividly with the hazy luminosity of the distance. In a sense, Claude can be said to have created the first rules of landscape painting: for many years Englishmen considered Claude's to be the only true form of landscape.

Figure 4   Claude, Erminia and the Shepherds, *oil (Photo supplied by the Arts Council of Great Britain; reproduced by courtesy of the Holkham Estate)*

---

[1]A *repoussoir* feature in a landscape picture is one that stands out from the middle and background of the composition by being in relief. The term is derived from the theatre – which is entirely appropriate, for Claude's art turned all of nature into a stage set.

Figure 5   Richard Wilson, Pastoral Scene in the Campagna, *oil (Ashmolean Museum, Oxford)*

Figure 6   Richard Wilson, The Valley of the Mawddach, *oil (Walker Art Gallery, Liverpool)*

8

The first British painter to be influenced directly by Claude's half factual, half ideal visions of Italy was Richard Wilson (1713/14–82) who spent much of the 1750s in Italy. Not only did Wilson actually imitate Claude, but he also adapted the biased perception which his study of Claude had given him, and treated his native Welsh landscape in a way that would be familiar to gentleman collectors who had been on the Grand Tour in Italy.

EXERCISE

What similarities do you see between the paintings by Claude and Wilson (pages 7 and 8)?

DISCUSSION

Clearly their pictures actually *look* similar, but why? Wilson was very much influenced by the example of Claude while he was in Italy (as indeed any painter of landscape would have been), and his way of seeing a landscape is precisely that of Claude. The subject matter is similar: Claude chooses an episode from Tasso, while Wilson chooses an unspecific pastoral scene with shepherds, the traditional population of a Claudian landscape. The compositions are similar: dark *repoussoir* features in the foreground contrast with the radiant distance. *Coulisses*[1] mark the progress into the distance, and in each picture there is an indefinable feeling of grace and well-being, hallmarks of this mode of landscape.

We have seen that so popular and affecting were the combination of Claude and Italy that they even biased the perception of a Welshman like Wilson who spent only a relatively little time in Italy. This idea of 'biased perception' is important to an understanding of how men see the world around them, because, in part, the achievement of painting in the age of industrialization was to get beyond the perceptual biases created by tradition.

What is perceptual bias? One of the best known examples occurs throughout Homer's vast epic of pre-classical antiquity, *The Odyssey*. Like the landscape painters who used Claude's formulas in landscape, so Homer himself borrowed the formulas of older, oral poets. One of these was the description of the sea as 'wine-dark'. Now, we do not know whether Homer really saw the sea as the same colour as wine, or whether he was just referring to its degree of darkness, but we do know that ancient Greek wine *was* very dark. Even if Homer had recognized that the sea was blue he would not have had a word to describe it: the Greek word for dark red also means dark blue! Perception develops in accordance with requirements. We have many more words to describe colours than there were, say, in the Middle Ages; it is said that Eskimoes have up to fifty different words to describe what we call snow, while their vocabulary is deficient when it comes to having to describe grass or an aeroplane. Now this would be merely an amusing diversion if the same phenomenon had not occurred among English artistic circles in the eighteenth century, the period when Claude pictures were being bought and when Richard Wilson was creating a market for himself. So much had Claude affected taste and the way that people saw the world that

a   All paintings of landscape had to look like Claude's pictures of Italy

b   English gardens were remodelled to look like Claude paintings

c   Most astonishing of all, gentlemen travelling in England took to carrying with them a plano-convex mirror, often coloured blue, which was known as a Claude Glass (see Figure 7).

---

[1]*Coulisses:* properly, in the theatre, sets at the side of the stage, but used in the terminology of landscape to describe those features of a picture which fit into one another in the pictorial distance to give the effect of space.

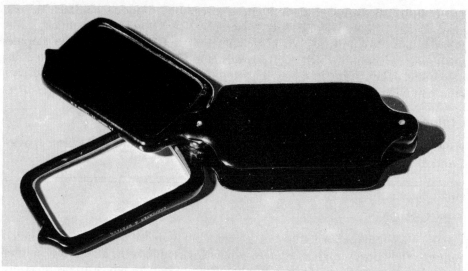

Figure 7   A Claude Glass (Crown copyright; Science Museum, London)

The Claude Glass was held up to reflect the English countryside as it passed the carriage window, and it then reflected the countryside *in a distorted way*, deforming the natural scene into a Claude-like composition with dark foreground features, tinged with the characteristic Claudian blue! For an English milord, scenery at home was just not worth seeing unless it was through the eyes of Claude. To be meritorious, nature had to imitate art.

This taste led to the aesthetic cult we call the 'picturesque'. The word is derived from the Italian *pittoresco* which means, literally, 'picture-like'. In picturesque art, landscape is not treated as a background detail, subservient to the main theme of a picture – as it was in say, the painting by Vecellio (Figure 2) – but as an autonomous vision of nature. The picturesque is an artificial mode because it demands the modification of nature according to artistic principles.

The most important figure in the picturesque movement was the writer and traveller, the Rev. William Gilpin. On his various travels, so anxious was Gilpin to apprehend nature 'picturesquely' that, when looking at a landscape, he would wriggle about to adjust the view so that it conformed to his abstract requirements, inspired by his knowledge of pictures. In his *Essay on Prints* (1768), Gilpin defined 'picturesque' as a 'term expressive of that peculiar kind of beauty, which is agreeable in a picture', and on his travels he had the opportunity fully to develop his knowledge of that kind of beauty. In the 1760s, of course, landscape paintings treated only rural themes and this conditioned Gilpin's distaste for cities. He wrote:

> London comes up apace; and all those disgusting ideas, with which its great avenues abound – brick-kilns steaming with offensive smoke – sewers and ditches sweating with filth – heaps of collected soil, and stinks of every denomination – clouds of dust, rising and vanishing, from agitated wheels, pursuing each other in rapid motion – or taking stationary possession of the road, by becoming the atmosphere of some cumbersome, slow moving wagon – villages without rural ideas – trees, and hedge-rows without a tinge of green – and fields and meadows without pasturage, in which loving bullocks are crowded together waiting for the shambles; or cows penned, like hogs, to feed on grains. It was an agreeable relief to get through this succession of noisome objects, which did violence to all the senses by turns: and to leave behind us the busy hum of men; stealing from it through the quiet lanes of Surrey; which leading to no great mart, or general rendezvous, affords calmer retreats on every side, than can easily be found in the neighbourhood of so great a town.
> (*Observations, Relative Chiefly to Picturesque Beauty*, pages 267–8)

Thus Gilpin, the picturesque traveller. His attitude to the town and the country is even more readily understandable when we recall that in the 1780s, before the appearance of suburbs which formed a 'grey' area between the urban and the rural, the contrast would have been immediate. Gilpin's attitude may well also have been conditioned by the rigours of travel in the late eighteenth century. His intention of searching after effects, which, by making the beautiful visible, enabled people to enjoy travel, may have been considered some sort of sop to the discomfort of gentlemen's carriages.

EXERCISE

Now read Essay II from Gilpin's *Three Essays* of 1792, reproduced in the Reader pages 25–9. What do you understand about Gilpin's attitude to beauty?

DISCUSSION

Gilpin's essay is written in archaic language but the ideas are simple enough. The essay is 'On Picturesque Travel' and was written as a guide to travellers to indicate what they could expect to get out of a journey. Gilpin's main points are these (not necessarily in this order):

1   Travel can be considered a pastime, an end in itself.

2   Its object is the discovery of beauty, whether natural or artistic.

3   The most important type of beauty is picturesque beauty, the sort of beauty which art teaches us to see in nature.

4   The traveller, intent on discussing picturesque beauty, must be prepared to modify nature with his imagination.

Gilpin's awareness of the picturesque was certainly an innovation in the history of taste, but it was short-lived because it was a highly artificial mode. However, the taste for looking at nature – even in such an artificial way – led to the creation of an entirely new way of seeing: *seeing clearly*. This was the fundamental achievement of painting in the early nineteenth century.

The development from picturesque landscape to the natural vision of a painter like John Constable is nothing less than the development of *man's ability to see*. It was, after all, only a few years after Gilpin was directing the picturesque travel-ler to squint and wriggle in order to make nature accommodate herself to some sort of pictorial ideal, that Constable, in the company of his early mentor, the painter and collector Sir George Beaumont, brought an old violin out of doors. Placing the brown instrument on the bright green grass, Constable was pleased to demonstrate that, obscured by layers of varnish, the brown foregrounds of the old master pictures hanging in gentlemen's collections all over the country were not accurate. Nature, Constable was suggesting, must be the source of art. In less than half a century the tables had been turned.

These units are divided into five main parts. The first part, which I have called 'Tremendous, Awful and Sublime', is about the first response by artists to a change in the accepted attitude to the country. In part it concerns the topog-raphical artists whose records of what they saw (which were always influenced by the picturesque mode) provide us with much of the raw material for an understanding of the attitude to landscape in the later eighteenth century. This part is also directly concerned with how different artists portrayed some of the central features of the early Industrial Revolution: the ironworks and mines. Two further sections deal with individual painters. One, Joseph Wright of Derby, also painted 'industrial' subjects and was the first to do so. The other, John Martin, painted no industrial scenes – indeed he painted no scenes ever observed on earth – but the scale and content of some of his pictures suggest that a major source of his inspiration came from the very real horrors of industry.

The second part is about John Constable, who set about, in his own words, to become a 'natural painter'. Constable rejected Gilpin's taste for stylized abstrac-tions and, in a mood characteristic of his times, set about to make painting into a science. Part 3 concerns Constable's great contemporary, J. M. W. Turner.

There follows an interlude where the writings of John Ruskin are briefly discussed. Ruskin was the champion of Turner and in his work there are echoes of all the major concerns of art (and, incidentally, society) in the middle nineteenth century.

For Ruskin also was the champion of the Pre-Raphaelite Brotherhood which is the subject of Part 4. This medievalizing 'brotherhood', which was formed in 1848, illustrates a current in art in the age of industrialization entirely different from the landscape tradition which was the subject of the first half of the century. The Pre-Raphaelites, typical of their times, wanted to create an art which, rejecting established conventions, looked back to a pre-industrial age of simplicity and honesty. Their art included criticism of contemporary society to a large degree. A version of their mass brand of social criticism found its most luxuriant expression in the (sometimes mawkish) work of the painters and graphic artists who followed them. These painters (Augustus Egg, Hubert von Herkomer, for instance) were the stuff of high Victorian art and are the subject of Part 5.

In the age of industrialization, art changed from an early phase, where the reality of nature was expressed by great painters who rid themselves of their constraining traditions, to a phase where themes of work, and the social detritus created by industrialization, combined to produce a suitable environment for an art which was critical of the conditions that led to its creation. It is the purpose of these units to trace the development of painting in England between these two phases.

1 TREMENDOUS, AWFUL AND SUBLIME

1.1 TRAVELLERS AND TOPOGRAPHERS

In the eighteenth century exploration and travel were among the chief intellectual pursuits. Through travel, and its record topography, poets and painters helped to create taste. While the rich and titled went to Italy and, perhaps, to Greece, on the Grand Tour, the less well-off had to stay at home and make what they would out of the native British scenery. We have already seen one example of this in Richard Wilson's *The Valley of the Mawddach* (Figure 6), a treatment of a British scene in the Italian taste; but English topography was also treated in a more direct way.

Figure 8   Samuel and Nathaniel Buck, North East Prospect of Richmond, *pen and ink and grey wash, 1745. This is one of the Bucks' original sketches from which engravings were made (Ashmolean Museum, Oxford)*

Few of the older topographical artists were men of great talent and few of them were English. From the seventeenth century, when the Bohemian artist Wenceslaus Hollar (1607–77) was in England, topographical art had often been in the hands of foreigners. Native English topography could be said to begin with the publication of *Buck's Antiquities,* volumes by Samuel (1696–1779) and Nathaniel (1727–53) Buck. These were collections of their engravings, sketched during summer travels and engraved in winter. *Buck's Antiquities,* however, was of more purely antiquarian than artistic interest. In an age when engraving was the only means of mass-producing images, the Bucks provided information on what England looked like that could be obtained nowhere else.

Figure 9   Samuel Scott, The Thames and the Tower of London on the King's Birthday, *oil, 1771 (Yale Center for British Art, Paul Mellon Collection)*

Samuel Scott (1702–72) was a far more accomplished artist than the Bucks. He specialized largely in marine pictures and the best are those which combine the sea with topographical details. His painting *The Thames and the Tower of London on the King's Birthday* (Figure 9) is such an example. It was probably the success of a foreigner, Canaletto, which motivated Scott to paint scenes like this one. Scott's work, like the Bucks', was pure observation untinged by any artistic temperament. In this sense it was good topography, if mediocre as an artistic experience.

Figure 10   Paul Sandby, Coal Winding Gear in a Rural Landscape, *watercolour (The National Museum of Wales, Cardiff)*

The first painter who combined an interest in topographical subject matter with real artistic merit was the Nottingham artist Paul Sandby (1725–1809). Sandby, who was a founder member of the Royal Academy and an artist employed by the Ordnance Survey, had an alert interest in the developments around him. Sandby painted early industrial scenes as well as pictures in watercolour which, while being topographically accurate, were charged with a sense of individual personality which the work of Scott and the Bucks lacked.

If Sandby was the finest exponent of the topographical tradition in British art then he was also its last. By the time of his death the tradition was effectively over. To see what replaced it, two works, one by Sandby and one by his eldest follower Michael 'Angelo' Rooker (1743–1801), may be compared.

EXERCISE

Look at Figure 11, Paul Sandby, *Castle Ruins*, and Figure 12, Michael 'Angelo' Rooker, *Buildwas Abbey*. Would you say that both of these pictures were topographical? (Write a paragraph or two on this question.)

DISCUSSION

If you looked at the pictures in terms of their general effect, you might have concluded that Sandby's painting is nearer to fantasy than to topography. It is not like a straightforward record of a place, but is a collection of all those different aspects of a scene which interested romantic landscape painters: storms, darkness, bold oppositions of light and shade, and the almost inevitable ruins. Sandby's picture is a work of the imagination. Rooker's painting, on the other

Figure 11 *Paul Sandby,* Stormy Sea with Castle Ruins and Figures in the Foreground, *gouache (City Art Gallery, Birmingham)*

Figure 12 *Michael 'Angelo' Rooker,* Buildwas Abbey, *watercolour, exhibited 1770 (Ashmolean Museum, Oxford)*

hand, is an accurate description of a real, individual monument. Yet Rooker still included some picturesque gypsies for effect and there appear to be two travelling gentlemen in the distance. Both pictures *extend* the topographical tradition by including picturesque details.

The need to extend the rather narrow boundaries of the topographical tradition was widely felt during the later eighteenth century. An accident of geography helped accomplish this because the usual routes of the picturesque traveller, going to Wales or the Lakes in search of views, took him through the new industrial areas which were developing in South Wales, the north-west and Midlands of England. Conditioned by that taste for the 'tremendous' and 'awful' which can be detected in Sandby's work, some travellers were drawn to the new centres of industry and felt compelled to share the experience of a mine or an iron forge at first hand. This was a period when art and industry (or science) shared similar concerns. There was little of the antagonism between art and industry which we detect today; an artist could be genuinely interested in the brave innovations of industry, for his attention had not yet been drawn to its evils. In his brilliant book on this era Francis Klingender called this a period of 'enchantment' (see 'Recommended Reading', page 75).

Enchanted tourists, with their eyes trained by art, were determined to descend pits and mines in conditions of shocking discomfort. A visitor to a salt-mine in Northwich, Cheshire, would expect to be loaned some miner's garb and be lowered some 200 feet in a bucket into the bowels of the earth. One tourist, embarking on his search for effects with a little trepidation, said on being lowered into a Cornish tin mine for the first time: 'It requires a good strong stomach, and a large portion of curiosity to go through with this' (Elspeth Moir, *The Discovery of Britain*, page 92).

Some mines even kept permanent guides to help tourists, and few were deterred by squalor or danger from chasing the effects of the mines. Often travellers were inspired to cite poetry as the nearest in effect to the new scenes of industry. The road between Walsall and Birmingham was said by one traveller to be not unlike Milton's Pandemonium in *Paradise Lost*, while others besides had recourse to the example of Milton as well as of Dante.

If this seems unlikely or eccentric, you should remember that poets themselves were not unimpressed. Thomas Gray could turn from the contemplation of a waterfall at one moment to a nearby iron forge at the next – for at the end of the eighteenth century, a natural waterfall *could* be next to an iron forge. Industry was in the country, not in the town, and this explains much of the travellers' enchantment with it. Out searching for a picturesque view suggested by Gilpin, a traveller might, at the same time, enjoy a demonic scene of early industry. But as soon as industry moved into the town, artists lost interest.

1.2   INDUSTRY IN ART: COALBROOKDALE AND CYFARTHFA

Coalbrookdale is popularly seen as the home of the Industrial Revolution – a view which is justified by events. It was here in the Severn Gorge in Shropshire that the father of a dynasty of iron-masters called Abraham Darby first smelted iron with coke in 1709. All things were propitious for such an invention for at Coalbrookdale there was a confluence of coal, ironstone and water, the three things necessary (before the age of easy and cheap transport) for ironworks to flourish. By 1742 Abraham Darby II had installed steam engines to drive the pumps and in 1779 Abraham Darby III, the most famous of them all, hired the architect, T. F. Pritchard, to build the Ironbridge. That bridge became a symbol of the Industrial Revolution (it was the first iron bridge to be built anywhere in the world), and the chief embellishment of Coalbrookdale. What a collection of attractions the area held for the traveller! Not only was it situated in a part of Shropshire which was naturally *picturesque* but there was also the most inspiring and vivid of industrial scenes. In his *Journals* Sir Joseph Banks described what he had seen there:

> While the Piggs are casting the Bellows are suffered to go but gently, but the small wind they occasion finding vent at the hole in the Furnace made for the dross to run over fills the room almost intirely full of sparks making a most beautiful appearance. The waste of the cinder before casting affords an appearance which gives the Idea of rivers of lava running down the sides of a volcano in an irruption. Streams of Liquid Fire issuing out from thence & dispersing different ways still run slower as they become cooler.
> (Elspeth Moir, *The Discovery of Britain*, page 99)

16

Sir Joseph's description (which was written in about 1767–8) is interesting because it combines an accurate technical appraisal with a passion for the visual effects. As early as the later 1760s such an account could not be matched by the visual arts. Some of the earliest views of Coalbrookdale are topographical ones which have no artistic personality. Such a picture is Figure 13, a pencil drawing which takes in all the details without making any comment on them.

Figure 13   Joseph Farrington, Coalbrookdale with Upper Forge and Pool, *pencil drawing, 1789 (Iron-bridge Gorge Museum Trust)*

The taste for the sublime soon caught up with Coalbrookdale when the eccentric painter Philip James de Loutherbourg (1740–1812) arrived there. De Loutherbourg had something of a reputation for the extravagant and the sublime and his picture of Coalbrookdale was among the first to represent the place in the modern style. The vigour of his treatment can be compared with a version of the identical scene by Paul Sandby.

EXERCISE

Look at Figure 14, Philip James de Loutherbourg, *Coalbrookdale at Night*, and Figure 15, Paul Sandby, *Bedlam Furnace, Madeley Dale, Shropshire* (overleaf). How do the two treatments of the same subject compare? Point out any differences you notice; for instance, does one artist express his experience with greater intensity than the other?

DISCUSSION

Both pictures are of the same scene, and both artists have chosen almost identical compositions, with the large group of buildings on the left, the path running through the centre of the scene and people placed in the middle ground to give the scale. De Loutherbourg's is, though, very much more *sublime* than Sandby's. He pays great attention to the intensity of the blaze at the furnace and has clearly enjoyed painting the sulphurous clouds of smoke escaping from the forge. Sandby's peasants and workmen appear to be loitering aimlessly in an almost picturesque scene, while de Loutherbourg's, particularly the two men with the horses and cart, appear agitated and overwhelmed by the tumultuous activity behind them. Both painters include derelict industrial artefacts as foreground

Figure 14   Philip James de Loutherbourg, Coalbrookdale by Night, *oil, c. 1800 (Photo supplied by the Science Museum, London; original painting is housed in the Science Museum)*

Figure 15   Paul Sandby Munn, Bedlam Furnace, Madeley Dale, Shropshire, *watercolour, 1803 (Photo by Douglas Smith. Private Collection)*

features, but de Loutherbourg's, in the dark of the night and reflecting as they do the orange heat of the furnace, are very much more menacing.

It is characteristic that the furnace portrayed in these paintings was known as 'Bedlam': to the connoisseur of the sublime, the chaos, noise and fury of the furnaces must have appeared in every way as exciting as the madhouse. But de Loutherbourg, too, produced some pastoral versions of similar subject matter. A coloured aquatint (Figure 16) shows a 'picturesque' peasant riding on horseback with derelict iron castings in the foreground, as in the night-time painting. But this time, these are more like crumbling mementoes of the picturesque than features designed horridly to contrast with the background.

There was another ironworks, too, which exercised the inspiration of many artists. This was Richard Crawshay's Cyfarthfa Works, near Merthyr Tydfil. The painter, Julius Caesar Ibbetson (1759–1817) spent some time at Cyfarthfa, considered the works 'stupendous' and produced a painting to prove it (Figure 17). J. M. W. Turner, in his early phase as a topographical artist, sketched there too, leaving us some of his drawings in a 'Cyfarthfa Sketchbook' now in the British Museum.

Figure 16   William Picket (after de Loutherbourg), Ironworks at Coalbrookdale, *aquatint,* c. 1792–1820 *(Ironbridge Gorge Museum Trust)*

Figure 17   Julius Caesar Ibbetson, Interior of Cyfarthfa Ironworks, *watercolour,* c. 1789 *(Cyfarthfa Castle Museum, Merthyr Tydfil. Photo by John Yates)*

Figure 18   J. M. W. Turner, Cyfarthfa Ironworks from the Brecon Road, *drawing, 1798 (Crown copyright. Reproduced by permission of the Trustees of the British Museum)*

Figure 19   Lucas van Valckenborgh, Mountain Landscape with Mine and Huts *(painting now attributed to Claes Dircksz van der Heck) (Rheinisches Landesmuseum, Bonn)*

Figure 20   Georgius Agricola, De Re Metallica, *Book VI, woodcut (also in Winkelmann,* Der Bergbau in der Kunst, *Essen, 1958, No. 131) (From a copy in Deutches Bergbau-Museum Bochum)*

Mines were another source of subject matter for painters. As a legitimate subject for paintings mines are the only industrial theme which has a pedigree in European art. There were pictures painted in the Middle Ages which showed *what people did*, like Figure 19, or technical illustrations to encyclopaedias like Figure 20, but these did little to suggest prototypes to modern artists who wanted to treat the theme of mining in their art. Julius Caesar Ibbetson painted a picture of the Parys Mine in Anglesey which showed miners being lowered to work in their buckets. For this he relied on the style which was already established in the later topographical tradition. His picture shows a fascination with the visually unusual; like the description which exists of the coal miners on Cannock Chase being surrounded by forests full of red deer, it reminds us that this was still the age of 'enchantment' of art with industry.

1.3 JOSEPH WRIGHT OF DERBY

Contemporary with the work of those painters who portrayed topographical scenes of the countryside showing some industrial activity, and with those (like de Loutherbourg) whose paintings seem to suggest menace, was Joseph Wright of Derby (1734–97).

Wright's career followed the conventional eighteenth-century course. He began as a portrait painter and his mature work was influenced by a period spent travelling in Italy. But it was in the period before his Italian journey (he left in 1773) that Wright painted a remarkable series of pictures of scientific, rather than industrial, subjects. Sometimes these pictures contain an element of traditional art, or of classical imagery, as though Wright were unwilling directly to present the world about him. An interpretation of Wright which leant too heavily on this idea would, however, be unjust. While some of Wright's paintings do look like the candle-lit scenes of certain seventeenth-century Dutch masters[1], they also

Figure 21   Joseph Wright of Derby, A Philosopher Giving a Lecture on the Orrery, *oil, c. 1764–6 (Derby Museum and Art Gallery)*

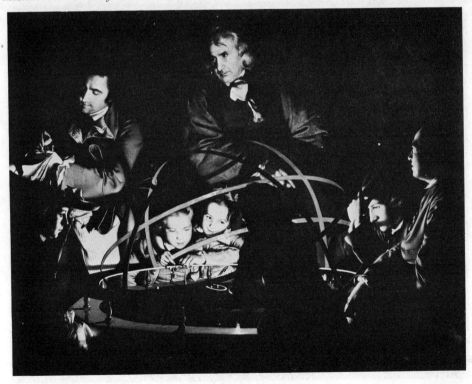

[1]Honthorst and Terbruggen, for example. At the same time, Georges de le Tour was painting similar scenes in France.

look rather like real-life demonstrations of scientific experiments which were then taking place in front of audiences of interested amateurs at various literary and philosophical institutions which were being set up around the country.[1]

Wright's two most well-known scenes of scientific experiment were painted within five years of each other. The first (Figure 21) was painted *c*. 1764–6. The composition of the picture is almost the same as that of a contemporary picture by Wright of some connoisseurs studying a piece of antique sculpture by candle-light. The picture is comparable to this more conventional theme in other ways too.

The orrery (named after the Earl of Orrery) was a device conceived to introduce the rudiments of planetary motion to the untutored. Wright has made the instrument just as much a centre of aesthetic attention as the antique sculpture in his painting of the connoisseurs, but the structure of the orrery gives him every bit as much opportunity to explore his painter's interest in formal relations and to display his skill in representing machine-finished surfaces.

What is going on? The philosopher, who stands in the middle of the composition, is explaining the motions of the planets to an audience which displays various degrees of interest in it. A young man on the left takes notes, while the young man on the right is listening attentively. Another young man on the right is staring, deep in concentration, at the workings of the machine. Two children are amused by the proceedings, while a young woman on the left looks a little bored. One person has his back to us. If you ask why Wright painted the scene by candlelight, the answer is that the orrery worked by the shadows cast by a bright lamp; but the drama of the demonstration, emphasized by this light–dark treatment, must also have appealed to Wright's temperament: his painting of the experiment with the orrery tells us much about science in the later eighteenth century. It was a private world, still somewhat full of mystery and fear and one which, by its very novelty, provided the painter with deliciously original subject matter.

Figure 22 Joseph Wright of Derby, An Experiment with a Bird in an Air-pump, *oil, c. 1767–8 (Tate Gallery, London)*

[1]Wright's friend, the poet Erasmus Darwin, was a member of such a body, The Lunar Society. Wright's professional work was also to bring him into contact with masters of industry such as the pottery master, Wedgwood and the cotton master, Arkwright.

The other well-known painting in this mode is Figure 22, *An Experiment with a Bird and an Air Pump.* Here the 'philosopher' leading the experiment is the anxious looking man in the background with his left hand raised. The experiment was designed to demonstrate how living creatures need oxygen. A bird (or sometimes a small mammal) was placed in the air-tight glass bowl and air was extracted until the creature was convulsed by a collapse of the lungs and appeared to die. At this point (and the timing had to be perfect, hence the philosopher's appearance of anxiety) air was reintroduced into the glass vessel and the bird or animal would revive, apparently miraculously. Wright has shown this rather cruel experiment having a harrowing effect on the audience which is divided into those who are either shocked or distraught, and those who patiently explain the scientific nature of the demonstration.

I think that these pictures are not moral allegories on the cruelty or dangers of science, but rather that they are examples of more-or-less precise observation. Despite the growing industry of the Midlands, not much of its direct influence was to be seen in the 1760s. Wright's pictures of these experiments are, in their own way, examples of *seeing clearly*. He is recording just that mystery and excitement which must have been felt at these experiments in darkened rooms – experiments which, like nature itself, had never been seen before. Wright caught and demonstrated the artistic potential of these scenes.

Science must have appeared to offer great and optimistic possibilities for the future to a man of the middle-classes like Wright, yet late in his life he was painting naturalistic landscapes. His *Landscape with a Rainbow* (Figure 23) uses dramatic effects of light. As Constable was to do later, Wright has caught that instant when the sun shines after a rain storm. The drama of his earlier work remains, but with this later picture Wright represents the end of scenes of industry and science in this phase of British art. The brief 'enchantment' was by now over.

Figure 23 Joseph Wright of Derby, View Near Chesterfield: Landscape with a Rainbow, *oil, c. 1794–5 (Derby Museum and Art Gallery)*

1.4   JOHN MARTIN AND HIS METROPOLITAN IMPROVEMENTS

Joseph Wright turned from painting scientific genre subjects to scenes of the natural countryside. This was seen as the loss of enchantment with science in favour of nature. In the paintings of John Martin we can see the expression of awe-struck wonder which a painter of the early nineteenth century showed on regarding the feats of industry. In *The Old Curiosity Shop*[1] Dickens had Little Nell and her father spending a fearful night by a great furnace. The taste is the same as Martin's: the tools and artefacts of industry are not sympathetic to human kind. In John Martin's paintings there is no feeling of 'enchantment': 'fear' would be a more appropriate word.

John Martin was born in 1789 and was thus younger than both Constable and Turner, but his art must be dealt with before theirs because it is of an earlier type. Factories, furnaces and mines ceased to be appropriate subjects for art as soon as it was generally realized that the workers who toiled in such infernal conditions were not the extras in a scene from Dante's *Inferno* or Milton's Hell, but real human beings brutalized by harsh labour. Furthermore, by the first quarter of the nineteenth century, industrial housing was widespread around the great manufacturing centres of the British Isles and industry had at last been divorced from the countryside with which it was once in harmony. Industrial touring in search of the picturesque, or the sublime, was no longer possible.

Figure 24   John Martin, The Great Day of His Wrath, *oil, 1852 (Tate Gallery, London)*

John Martin's art can be seen as a realization of that nineteenth-century morality which began to question the ethics of industry. It is hard to imagine that *The Great Days of His Wrath* (Figure 24) was not influenced by a tour of the Black Country. Of this picture his son, Leopold, wrote

> The glow of the furnaces, the red blaze of light, the liquid fire seemed to his mind dryly sublime and awful. He could not imagine anything more terrible, even in the regions of everlasting punishment. All he had done, or attempted in ideal painting, fell far short, very far short, of the fearful sublimity of effect when the furnaces could be seen in the full blaze in the depth of night.
> (Leopold Martin in Mary Pendered, *John Martin, Painter, His Life and Times,* page 248)

[1]Chapter XLIV.

Figure 25   John Martin, The Bridge over Chaos, *mezzotint (Crown copyright. Victoria & Albert Museum)*

EXERCISE

Look at Figure 25, a mezzotint by John Martin called *The Bridge Over Chaos.* What do you 'see' in this picture?

DISCUSSION

The mezzotint is a representation of Sin and Death building a bridge over Chaos (an incident from Milton's *Paradise Lost*). If you did not know this (and you could not be expected to), you could see that Martin has depicted a scene which gives the viewer a thrilling impression of depth and infinity. There is also a feeling of mystery and fear which is suggested by the pervasive darkness. The characters (we must not, after all, call them 'people') are very small indeed, quite dwarfed by the majesty of their setting. It is the work of a man with a powerful imagination. It may come as no surprise to you that John Martin had an insane brother who attempted to burn down York Minster. In *The Bridge over Chaos* John Martin barely controls a tottering artistic sanity. The impression is that a wild, colossal vision had been tamed just enough to get it into the four straight edges of a picture.

If this were just the fantastic depiction of a scene from Milton, it would be interesting as an example of the morbid sublimity which seized some artists in the first half of the last century. But if you look again at *The Bridge over Chaos* you will see that the 'bridge' is actually leading into a tunnel. Coincidentally, at the same time as Martin was illustrating Milton, one of the grandest failures of nineteenth-century engineering was being undertaken in London: the Thames Tunnel. Work was begun on the tunnel in 1828, amid a certain public disquiet concerning the safety of the operation. An underground banquet was held in the works in 1827 to reassure the public. Only a short while after the banquet the walls collapsed and the tunnel was not completed until 1843. It is tempting to see in Martin's picture some expression of the public awe at such a fearful enterprise which seemed almost to have usurped the Creator's role, for Martin's *The Bridge over Chaos* looks very much like contemporary illustrations of the Thames Tunnel!

The Mirror
OF
LITERATURE, AMUSEMENT, AND INSTRUCTION.

No. 809.]   SATURDAY, DECEMBER 10, 1836.   [Price 2*d.*

THE THAMES TUNNEL.—I

THE WESTERN ARCHWAY.

Figure 26 The Western Archway, Thames Tunnel, *engraving, 1836 (Photo supplied by Mary Evans Picture Library)*

In the paintings of John Martin we can see many of the effects and motifs which nineteenth-century industry provided, but all the time cloaked in a disguise afforded by a literary or biblical theme. Martin's *Pandemonium* (Figure 27 – another scene from Milton) looks as if it might have been illuminated by gas-mantles.

Figure 27 John Martin, Pandemonium, 1841, *mezzo tint (Collection: H. B. Huntingdon-Whiteley. Photo by City Art Gallery, Birmingham)*

Yet, if Martin appears to be exorcizing the diabolical influences of industry by dressing up the effects as theatre, an argument can be made to suggest that he influenced the technical and engineering works of his own time. Some of his grander architectural fantasies such as *Belshazzar's Feast* (Figure 28), an imitation of the ancient wonders of the world, may have influenced, of all people, the railway engineers.

Figure 28 John Martin, Belshazzar's Feast, *mezzotint, c. 1821 (Crown copyright. Reproduced by courtesy of the Trustees of the British Museum)*

Figure 29 H. Pyall (after Thomas Talbott Bury), Entrance of the Railway at Edge Hill, *aquatint, 1831 (City of Manchester Art Galleries)*

Compare Figure 28, *Belshazzar's Feast* with Figure 29, *Entrance of the Railway at Edge Hill*. Certainly, the suggestion is not that the railway engineers making the cutting into Liverpool's Lime Street Station were consciously taking their inspiration from John Martin; but rather, that the mode of expression devised by John Martin to represent the ancient world passed into the general consciousness of the nineteenth century, and that his architecture of the magnificent ancient world found a new home in some of the architecture of the magnificent new world which engineering had realized.

But Martin's imagination extended into the outside world in a more tangible form. Martin was an early example of the artist with a social conscience. Indeed, it would be possible to write an account of art in the age of industrialization which dwelt solely on the artist's concern for society. John Martin, besides making pictures, wanted to do little else but improve the capital city. The idea of *improving* London had been in the air for a long time.[1]

In the days when London's water supply was in the hands of private companies and when cholera was a very real scourge, John Martin had published plans for diverting sewage from the river and using it profitably as manure. In 1829, he proposed plans for a weir running across the Thames. He made additions to these plans throughout the 1830s and 1840s. All these, characteristically, came to nothing. He wrote:

> . . . Though I have reaped no advantage, I have, at least, the satisfaction of knowing that the agitation thus kept up constantly, solely by myself, has resulted in a vast alteration in the quantity and quality of water supplied by the companies.
> (Pendered, *John Martin the Painter*, page 197)

Martin, as well as being interested in water works and sewage, proposed a dock railway connecting with the main lines; various schemes for lighthouses; designs for anchors and cables; ventilation for coal mines (very much an issue of the times); floating harbours and iron ships. All Martin's grand schemes were directed to 'improvement' and to health, two goals which the power of industry flattered the public that it could provide, but in the end deceived it by providing neither.

These schemes of Martin's showed that the visionary powers of the artist might be made useful. His was an attempt to combine science and the arts. The next artist whose work we are going to look at tried to make art into a science.

---

[1]The town planning schemes which the architect John Nash had carried out for the Prince Regent had done much to stimulate the popular imagination. Influenced by Nash, another architect, James Elmes, had written a book called *Metropolitan Improvements* in 1829 and in 1855 the Metropolitan Board of Works was set up.

2 JOHN CONSTABLE: THE NATURAL IDYLL

2.1 CONSTABLE'S ACHIEVEMENT

Constable 1776–1837 made art into a 'science' by studying nature in depth, following its moods and training himself to capture its momentary appearance. In doing this he broke completely with the classical tradition of landscape and, although some of his early pictures[1] are derived from Claude, his great achievement was to bring nature down to earth. After Constable, no artist, except perhaps the occasional hack, would ever attempt to paint a formalized, classical landscape. Constable's innovations of vision were one of the direct precursors of modern art; his example required all subsequent painters of standing to see the world more and more directly, as if they were scientific observers. Constable's gradual discovery of appearances', as Roger Fry later called it, was one of the major intellectual developments of the nineteenth century.

Of all the things Constable said or wrote there might appear to be special contradictions between the following: 'Painting is a science'; 'Painting is for me but another word for feeling'; and 'There is room enough for a natural painter' – but in fact, all these statements of artistic intent mean the same thing. 'Natural philosophy' was the vogue term in the early nineteenth century for the scientific observation of nature; many of the great discoveries in botany and geology, for instance, were made by amateurs whose sole 'scientific' qualification was that they were very observant of nature. Constable, too, was very observant of nature, so his art could be considered natural philosophy and, thus, in the contemporary usage, his *art* was also a *science*!

We know well enough that Constable was concerned with natural philosophy because his letters give us evidence of the workings of his mind. In 1835 he even said that the sciences interested him more than the other arts. This enthusiasm for science may have something to do with the practicality of Constable's personality. What is so very interesting about this is that the practical, 'scientific', observant character he developed estranged him from the conventions of contemporary art and the company of contemporary artists; yet it was this very practicality which, in the first place, brought about his Wordsworthian surrender to nature. He subdued his consciousness and allowed his eye fully to absorb, without prejudiced foreknowledge, and fully to discover the appearance of the world; but like Wordsworth, he also fully discovered what we might call the moral truth of the landscape.

Late in his life, when delivering a lecture to the Hampstead Literary and Scientific Society, Constable summarized his art. He said:

> In such an age as this, painting should be *understood*, not looked on with blind wonder, nor considered only as poetic aspiration, but as a pursuit, *legitimate, scientific and mechanical.*
> (R. B. Beckett, *John Constable's Discourses*, Suffolk Records Society, vol. 14, page 69)

The last four words are extraordinary, yet very fitting to the age and also to Constable's art.

EXERCISE

Look at Figure 30 (overleaf), John Constable, *Weymouth Bay*. What is there in it of direct observation?

---

[1]For instance, the *Dedham Vale* of 1802 in the Victoria and Albert Museum.

Figure 30   John Constable, Weymouth Bay, *oil, 1816 (Crown copyright. Victoria & Albert Museum)*

DISCUSSION

In this picture Constable has tried to capture *effect*, and in so doing has abandoned detail. Natural colour and light have been accurately observed and the painter has captured the appearance of swirling clouds and misty air on an unsettled day. The figures in the middle-ground (who clearly do not much interest Constable) are dealt with in only the sketchiest of manners, but their importance as a part of the pictorial composition is significant: they contrast vividly with the bright patch of sunlight which the painter has shown sweeping across the beach. You might also have noticed that Constable avoids the *repoussoir*, and other Claudian devices.

In his pictures Constable showed the world what had always existed in nature, but what had seldom been seen before. One of his means of achieving this was by meditating long and hard on the subject of a painting, absorbing every detail and every changing effect. Sometimes many years elapsed between the original sketch and the finished, painted-up composition which would be exhibited (see Figures 31a and 31b). It is not known when Constable painted the picture of the cottage, but it is clear from the documentary evidence that the canvas went through a series of 'touch-ups' before it was finally exhibited at the Royal Academy in 1833.

Now this 'scientific' attitude to nature is doubly interesting if you recall what was said before about natural 'philosophy' in the late eighteenth and early nineteenth centuries. Constable's natural science was very much a characteristic of his age: he gave a course of lectures at the Royal Institution and there he might have been expected to bump into Faraday and Davy. If you remember that chemistry was as popular a subject for young ladies as was sketching, then it will come as no surprise to think of Constable in the way he wished to be considered: as a natural scientist (or 'philosopher').

How far did Constable's 'science' extend? His idea of natural philosophy was predicted by exceptional figures in the eighteenth century; even the great French academician, Roger de Piles, had said that Claude painted as though he knew physics. Yet this idea of seeing things clearly and sorting them into categories

Figure 31a   John Constable, Cottage in a Cornfield, *drawing, c. 1815 (Crown copyright. Victoria & Albert Museum)*

Figure 31b   John Constable, Cottage in a Cornfield, *oil, exhibited 1833 (Crown copyright. Victoria & Albert Museum)*

was a peculiarly nineteenth-century one. What Constable did for nature, through art, was paralleled by a London chemist Luke Howard, in his work on clouds: Howard's book, *The Climate of London* (1818–20) established all the basic cloud types which we still recognize today. Howard's work had impressed Goethe who praised him, like Linnaeus, for putting a form on what had hitherto been indeterminate. In the same way as Constable's paintings had made facile, rule-bound conventions of landscape impossible for thinking artists, so had Howard's scientific observation of the weather made merely amateur observation impossible.

When Howard wrote his book, meteorology was still very much an upstart subject, an *arriviste* among the sciences, not nearly as popular among ladies of taste as chemistry or astronomy. Constable – despite the beguiling idea that he might have painted his clouds in imitation of a scientific text – apparently knew little about Howard's work, although he did know Thomas Forster's *Researches about Atmospheric Phenomena,* and Forster had been a pupil of Howard's. Interestingly, although they appear convincing, Constable's clouds are not always correctly matched to the terrain over which they are shown!

If Constable was keeping a 'scientific' eye on the weather, what was happening to the countryside around him? It would be misleading to think of Suffolk as a quaint, agricultural backwater for there was industry of sorts in Suffolk. Constable's pictures include mills (his father was a miller and perhaps the family tradition helped Constable develop his acute eye, for millers are forever aware of the changes in the weather), canal scenes and boatyards (his father owned one of these, too). If Constable's Suffolk pictures appear to us tranquil and idyllic we should remember that these are, in their own way, scenes of nineteenth-century industry which show the pace of life in a lightly industrialized area. The changes in the actual appearance of the countryside between the mid-eighteenth and early nineteenth centuries were among the most remarkable phenomena to occur during the age of industrialization. In his Suffolk pictures Constable shows us much of what 'art' and 'manual toil', as one poet put it, were doing to the country.

During the second half of the eighteenth century, agriculture began to develop from the medieval practice of mere subsistence-farming into an organized, legislated and industrialized business. New implements were developed and new types of ploughs, seed-drills, threshers and reapers appeared. Constable was fascinated by the new machinery of agriculture; there is a whole group of his notes and sketches devoted to agricultural machinery. His countryside was industrial landscape.

Figure 32   John Constable, Study of Two Ploughs, 1814 *(Crown copyright. Victoria & Albert Museum)*

It was not only machinery which was altering the face of the countryside, but legislation as well. During the later eighteenth century the old system of common fields was abandoned in favour of enclosed fields. The effects of enclosure, speeded by Acts of Parliament throughout the century, were most keenly felt in north-east England, the Midlands and Constable's East Anglia. Instead of the old scene of open, unhedged landscape there appeared, in the interests of efficiency, geometrical fields divided by rough hawthorn hedges. Many of the copses and woods we see today are not old-established growths, but were late eighteenth- or early nineteenth-century plantings designed to be covers for game in the new landscape.

This enclosure movement gave England its present appearance, the one we are all too ready to regard as having been eternal. It is rewarding to think that Constable's way of seeing nature afresh parallels exactly the Englishman's first experience of organizing the face of the earth. It reminds us, also, that agriculture was the oldest industry. An agricultural commissioner and poet, Thomas Bachelor, wrote in precisely those terms. Bachelor's views on the changes occurring in the countryside were equivocal: his poem 'The Progress of Agriculture' is by no means strident in its support of progress. He thought of taming what he called the 'obdurate soil' and of creating wealthy new cities, but he was also sensible of the social effects of enclosure:

> But industry, thy unremitting hand
> Has changed the formless aspects of the land.
> To distant fields no more the peasants roam,
> Their cottage-lands and farms surround their home;
> And hawthorn fences, stretched from side to side,
> Contiguous pastures, meadows, fields divide . . .
> (Thomas Bachelor, from *Village Scenes, The Progress of Agriculture and Other Poems*, page 82)

EXERCISE

Re-read this short quotation from Bachelor's 'The Progress of Agriculture'. What are its most striking features?

DISCUSSION

1 Bachelor calls the enclosure movement 'industry'. He might not have meant it in exactly our modern sense, but his usage is an interesting one which gives us a good idea of the currency of the word in the early nineteenth century.

2 By writing of the *hitherto* 'formless' Bachelor suggests an improvement due to enclosure.

3 Similarly, he suggests that enclosure has benefited peasants because they don't have to go to far-away fields to work. (One of the most direct effects of enclosure was to create what we might today call 'smallholdings', a cottage surrounded by fields of its own.)

Later in the poem Bachelor develops his argument, writing that monopolies were ruining the land and the prosperity of the countryfolk, but even then his commitment to progress did not allow him to censure the new developments. In writing

> I ask not Science to withdraw her hand
> Nor hoary custom still to rule the land,

Bachelor demonstrates his faith in the future and his rejection of old values. He might have been a little shaken at the speed of the changes (this was the period, too, when new roads were being cut across the country), but he was convinced that the overall effect was beneficial. Constable's achievement was to capture in his pictures not only that instantaneous moment when the light changes, but also that relatively short historical moment when the face of Britain changed from being predominantly rural to being predominantly industrial.

2.2 CONSTABLE'S ART

Perhaps it was a memory of Suffolk in his early youth (he was born in 1776), when the county had yet been little affected by the revolutions in agriculture, that made Constable see it as a place of tranquillity, where rural and industrial arts were at one with nature. This quality, which the Suffolk countryside suggested to him, reminds us of the meditative nature of Constable's reaction to a scene: it was said that he would sit and stare, enchanted, at a given view or detail until all its parts were known to him. This part of his artistic character led many critics to compare his work to Wordsworth's. Certainly there is a community of feeling between much of Wordsworth's poetry and much of Constable's painting:

> To every natural form, rock, fruit, or flower,
> Even the loose stones that cover the highway,
> I gave a moral life.
> ('Prelude' III)

Constable too, had a pantheistic reaction to nature; he was angered to see a favourite tree violated by having a notice nailed on to it. In Coleridge's work there is a similar sense of nature being all-powerful. In this case, nature takes over from the church:

> So will I build my altar in the fields,
> And the blue sky my fretted dome shall be.
> ('To Nature', 1815)

While Constable shares with these great romantic poets a common sense of the power of nature, it is interesting to note that he enjoyed more the works of lesser poets. James Thomson, for instance, whose poem 'The Seasons', a work of middling quality, was vastly influential, inspiring Haydn. Robert Bloomfield, the local Suffolk poet, was the author of pastoral-sounding pieces like *The Farmer's Boy*, *Rural Tales* and *Love of the Country*. This last poem reminds us of Constable's words: 'Painting is for me but another word for feeling'. It begins thus:

> Welcome silence! welcome peace!
> O most welcome, holy shade!
> Thus I prove, as years increase,
> My heart and soul for quiet made.
> Thus I fix my firm belief
> While rapture's gushing tears descend,
> That every flower and every leaf
> Is moral Truth's unerring friend.
> (*Wildflowers; or Pastoral and Local Poetry*, page 89)

Novelty was a fundamental part of these romantic attitudes to the world and to artistic creation, but to Constable the art of the past was also a strong influence. He had a vivid sense of tradition and said, for instance, that Claude summarized everything he wanted to do in landscape. Seeing the work of other painters in nature itself is a characteristic of the picturesque mode. Constable was always doing it: he had even spoken of Richard Wilson's spirit walking arm-in-arm with Milton and Linnaeus. But, despite his awareness of the past, Constable's own spirit walked alone.

Let's look at a characteristic picture: *The Cornfield* (Figure 33). You can 'read' a Constable picture, the details being so precise and well-observed. The painting shows a lane leading from East Bergholt (Constable's own village) to the path

Figure 33 John Constable, The Cornfield, *oil, 1826 (National Gallery London)*

from Dedham (a village nearby). The church, strange to say for Constable, is a pure invention, but the meteorological observations were on this occasion precise. He wrote in his notebook:

> . . . Inland – cornfields – a Close lane – kind of a thing – but it is not neglected in any part. The trees are more than usually studied and the extremities well defined – as well as their species – they are shaken by a pleasant and healthfull breeze – 'at Noon'.
> (cited in Martin Davies, *The British School*, National Gallery Catalogue, page 10)

This makes a telling contrast with the bland, formalized abstractions of Claude's landscapes.

The Cornfield was exhibited at the Royal Academy in 1826 and at the Paris Salon in the following year. It is painted with just as much attention to precise observation as any other of his mature works. It appears to have been painted directly from nature. Or does it?

EXERCISE

Can you detect any other quality, or content, in *The Cornfield* which suggests that it was not just painted from nature?

DISCUSSION

At first sight *The Cornfield* looks to be painted entirely from observation of the countryside, but if you have looked at it closely you should have noticed a number of details which are contrived, or not taken purely from observation. For instance, I have already mentioned that the distant church tower is an invention and exists in the painting purely for pictorial reasons. The details you should have spotted include the drinking boy (which was, incidentally, Constable's preferred title for the picture), huntsmen in the distance, workmen half hidden in a cornfield and animals. Constable may have added all these details to his picture to make it into an allegory, representing, perhaps, the chain of existence which stretches from the innocent animals through the boy and workmen to the church in the distance, a symbol of life to come.

A picture like this can be interpreted on a number of different levels. Not only is there the suggestion of allegorical content, but Constable also derived elements of his picture from the art of the past: the motif of a boy drinking from a stream was a favourite one among eighteenth-century genre painters, while the treatment of the distant landscape is certainly indebted to the example of Claude.

Even if he borrowed from tradition, the synthesis which Constable made was entirely novel. He might always have had in mind Titian, Claude or Rembrandt, but nature was his real guide and he studied its intricacies so that he could master it. This brought Constable little success, for few of his contemporaries were equipped to appreciate his achievement. Constable was not an ambitious man, but he was anxious that this lack should be remedied and, accordingly, he set out, quite late in his life (1830–32), to publish a series of prints of his landscape paintings, which was to be known as *English Landscape*.[1] Although many other painters in other ages had had engravings made from their paintings, this was the first time that a painter had decided to publish his own novel visions of landscape and thereby give a degree of popular currency to his revolutionary view of the world around him. The mezzotints gave a uniform size and appearance to what had hitherto been an uncollected group of paintings of different shapes and sizes. This form of mechanical reproduction was as sophisticated as could be managed in the 1830s.

The engraver chosen by Constable for this important job was David Lucas (1802–81). In fact, the series was not at all successful though it continued after Constable's death. As a distillation of his own experience, of the scientific observation of nature, it was a great success, but as the justification of his life and his work to his peers, which he had intended it to be, it was a miserable failure.

In the prints from *English Landscape* like *Stoke-by-Nayland* (Figure 34) Constable used his favourite artistic principle, what he called the 'chiaroscuro of nature', to achieve the effect which he sought, which Wordsworth had called the capture of brief moments 'from fleeting time'. We are lucky in having preserved Constable's own specially composed commentary for this print. He wrote:

> The solemn stillness of Nature in a Summer's Noon, when attended by thunder-clouds, is the sentiment attempted in this print; at the same time an endeavour has been made to give an additional interest to this Landscape by the introduction of the Rainbow.

Constable's 'chiaroscuro of nature' was the sometimes sudden change between dark and light which, if it can be captured in a picture, gives the effect of moving light. It was perhaps because of motion, this most advanced of painterly features, that *English Landscape* failed to become popular. Constable's daughter was eventually left with over 4,000 separate prints to dispose of after his death.

---

[1] In fact called *Various Subjects of Landscape, Characteristic of English Scenery, from Pictures Painted by John Constable, RA,* it appeared in five parts, twenty prints altogether.

Figure 34   David Lucas (after John Constable), Stoke-by-Nayland, *mezzotint, 1830 (Fitzwilliam Museum, Cambridge)*

2.3   CONSTABLE: CONCLUSION

Constable created our notions of what the English landscape looked like, and he did so at a time when the landscape was going through some fundamental changes. Although he was aware of a great tradition of landscape art which went before him, Constable remains popular because no historical imagination or knowledge is necessary to appreciate his art. It speaks to us directly.

Perhaps this was why the great critic John Ruskin did not like him. Ruskin said that Constable

> . . . perceives in a landscape that the grass is wet, the meadows flat and the boughs shady; that is to say, about as much as, I suppose, might in general be apprehended, between them, by an intelligent fawn and a skylark.

Constable fared badly with the other critics too. He compared the contemporary art world with the Battle of Waterloo. To achieve his astonishing effects of directness Constable used what his contemporaries considered to be a too sketchy technique. Constable was hurt by his lack of acceptance,[1] but he painted only for himself. What he created, in his singular dedication to the capture of appearances, was one of the greatest innovations in the history of art. While John Martin had been recreating Babylon, John Constable had been looking around.

---

[1]He was only elected an Associate of the Royal Academy at forty-three, and even then there was a widely held belief that he had been lucky.

3 J.M.W. TURNER: THE NATURAL EPIC

3.1 TURNER AND THE WORLD ABOUT HIM

The scale and range of Turner's paintings was altogether different from Constable's: it was the epic compared to the idyll.

Joseph Mallord William Turner (1775–1851) was an immensely fertile and successful artist (he left over £140,000 at his death). The contrast with Constable could not be more complete. Constable's fresh, natural pictures shocked the Royal Academy, while Turner's steamy, evanescent scenes from ancient history and wars at sea (conceived on a scale as grand as John Martin's) satisfied the Academy's taste for the heroic. Constable's was a narrow range of subject; he restricted himself generally to the pursuit and capture of the *genius loci* while, on the other hand, Turner would paint anything. In their techniques the two could not have been more different: Constable was concerned with clarity and the study of pictorial structure, while Turner was more interested in the play of colour on the surface of the canvas. Lastly, Constable was a gifted writer of great eloquence, while Turner was nearly inarticulate. Yet it would be false to infer from this that he was merely a talented imbecile capable only of pleasing the Academicians. He managed much more than that: John Ruskin, the greatest critic of the day, became his champion (although they met as late as 1837) and helped Turner achieve a popularity and respect as vast as his visions of Carthage or the Alps.

The breadth of Turner's technique and the range of his interests were enormous, but while Sir Arthur Elton[1] (a noted authority on the Industrial Revolution) considered that in Turner's paintings we can see a treatment of industrial themes in a systematic way, I think it is fairer to see Turner as an eclectic, an artist who would draw his source from whatever pleased him. The changing landscape of nineteenth-century England was not, after all, his sole stimulus. Many of his better paintings were inspired by journeys abroad. But while industrial subject matter did supply him with some images, Turner should be seen as a partisan to no cause. In a sense, he was a painter of everyday life, drawing his inspiration no less from a furnace than from a castle, from a farm no less than a railway.

What was Turner like? We have a number of different accounts on which to base our interpretation of his character. His contemporary biographer, Walter Thornbury, said in his book (which, when it appeared was widely considered an attack on Turner) that the

> . . . demi-god was only a little, ignoble man, with sordid views and low tastes, who lived the life of a soured miser and suspicious recluse.
> (Walter Thornbury, *The Life of J. M. W. Turner, RA*)

To which a more modern biographer has added:

> The few whose hearts warmed to him had to turn a blind eye to his secretive and uncongenial habits, his utter lack of social graces, his distastes, bordering almost on mania, for all forms of hospitality, his furtive, often bewildering disappearances from England, and, last, but not least, his gruff, monosyllabic way of answering polite and inoffensive questions, to the thin-skinned tantamount to rudeness.
> (Bernard Falk, *Turner, the Painter: His Hidden Life*, page 124)

At the same time, Constable considered him 'uncouth', but paid tribute to his 'wonderful range of mind'.

[1] In *Art and the Industrial Revolution*, (1968) Exhibition Catalogue, City Art Gallery, Manchester.

We know about the house which Turner once lived in from Leopold Martin, John Martin's son. He said:

> The house was a gloomy, detached, five-windowed, large-doored abode. An extensive studio occupied the back of the residence . . . Mr Turner hardly struck one as a man who was producing works so full of poetry and art. His dress was certainly not that of a refined gentleman and painter. A loose body coat, very open side-pockets, with a dirty paint rag stuck in one of them; loose trousers, unbraced, and hanging under the heels of his slippers; a large rosewood palette on his thumb with a very big bunch of brushes of various sizes in his hand, and a rather old hat on his head . . . The studio was dark and gloomy, in every way like that of an untidy man, and not at all what one would have expected from so great a painter.
> (Pendered, *John Martin, Painter, His Life and Times*, page 85)

Many accounts also exist of Turner's competitiveness, his behaviour at varnishing days at the Academy and his attitude to his contemporaries. Some said that he mixed his colours with stale beer,[1] some that he was sociable, others that he was not. One thing is certain, Turner did not like Constable. In 1822 a painting by Constable (in fact, his *Opening of Waterloo Bridge)* was hung by a rather quiet, grey seascape by Turner. Constable's picture was a very colourful composition indeed, with lots of gold effects and vermilion details. Turner was incensed that Constable was attracting more attention than himself. Thornbury says

> Turner stood behind him (Constable) looking from the 'Waterloo' to his own picture; and, putting a round daub of red lead, somewhat bigger than a shilling, on his grey sea, went away without a word. The intensity of the red lead, made more vivid by the coolness of his picture, caused even the vermilion of Constable to look weak . . . 'He has been here', said Constable, 'and fired off a gun'.
> (Thornbury, *The Life of J. M. W. Turner, RA*, page 327)

Why should the man with perhaps the most visionary style of painting to appear in the whole of the nineteenth century have resorted to this detestable (if skilful) trickery, particularly against a painter like Constable, who enjoyed little of Turner's popular acclaim? Perhaps it had something to do with his tragic life, a sensibility which affects the whole of his art. Whatever the case, it is a salutary lesson that great art is not always the product of great men.

How does Turner fit into his age? Surely not just as the soured old hermit who could out-paint Constable; Turner was more than that, for he saw Europe with the eyes of a romantic. The scale of his vision was immense, yet like Constable, he saw England as it had never been seen before.

3.2   TURNER'S ART

We might expect that an artist who produced such original work as Turner must have been guided to his end by an elaborate theory of art, with his aims and intentions clearly defined. But this was not so. Turner had no specific theory. We know what he read and in so far as his attitude to art had a literary basis, we can draw some conclusions from what we know about the remains in his library. Throughout his life Turner was interested in imagery and in associations which words might fire off: words were always important to him and he used them freely to enhance the effect of his pictures.[2] Strangely though, apart from Byron, Turner had little time for his contemporary poets. He was more interested in Milton, Macpherson's *Ossian*, (a poem in an archaic style), Pope's *Iliad* and George Crabbe.

[1] Robert Leslie, for instance, whose account of Turner at varnishing day is reprinted in *Turner: Imagination and Reality*, Museum of Modern Art, New York, 1966, page 42.

[2] Turner's use of words as a supplement to his own art has been, with some justice, compared to that of Beethoven by J. R. Watson, 'Turner and the Romantic Poets' in *Encounters*, edited by John Dixon Hunt, Studio Vista, 1968.

Perhaps this was because he was rather insensitive to the poet's art and was more interested in content than style. This theory would be supported by Turner's own poetry which at best is only doggerel and at worst shows a shocking lack of sensitivity for the dignity of the language. Thornbury reproduces some lines of Turner's verse in his biography:

> To that kind Providence that guides our step
> Fain would I offer all that my power holds (?)
> And hope to be successful in my weak attempt
> To please. The difficulty great, but, when nought
> Attempted, nothing can be wrought,
> Though (?) thankful for the mental powers given,
> Whether innate or the gift of Heaven.
> (Walter Thornbury, *The Life of J. M. W. Turner, RA*, page 205)

– to which he adds that this extract 'will convince even the most sanguine enthusiast of the utter hopelessness of the painter's ever attaining to the rank of great poet'.

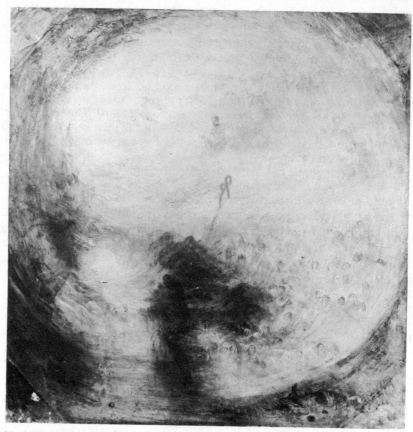

Figure 35   J. M. W. Turner, Light and Colour (Goethe's Theory): the Morning after the Deluge, *oil, 1843 (Tate Gallery, London)*

Turner's reading, as his art, was eclectic. There is one painting only, his *Light and Colour (Goethe's Theory) the Morning after the Deluge* (Figure 35), which hints at a contemporary *scientific* theory of art. Turner had read Goethe's *Zur Farbenlehre* (On the Theory of Colour), but this is more likely to be mere name-dropping than a representation of Goethe's science of colour.

If an organized theory of art did not play a part in Turner's astonishing career as a painter, how then did he manage so successfully to better himself and his contemporaries? I shall summarize briefly his development as a painter and then look at a couple of pictures in some detail.

Turner's earliest paintings, of the late 1790s and early 1800s, are all topographical: it was some time before he developed his uniquely personal vision of the world. Some of the early topographical works are charged with a strong sense of the pastoral – a sense, influenced by the tradition of art, that life in the country represented an ideal type of existence. Such a picture is Figure 36, *View on Clapham Common*. The subject is unremarkable (in 1800 Clapham was a village on the outskirts of London) and it is painted with a smudgy technique in earth colours; more attention has been paid to the general effect than to the particular detail. Perhaps this characteristic is a harbinger of what was to come in Turner's art: a concentration on the magnificent instead of the anecdotal. A similar picture is Figure 37, *Guildford from the Banks of the Wey*, which hints at Claude's formalized type of composition but whose colour values are entirely different, the luminous blues and greys of Claude being replaced by dark, wet-looking earth colours.

Figure 36   J. M. W. Turner, View on Clapham Common, *oil, c. 1800–5 (Tate Gallery, London)*

Figure 37   J. M. W. Turner, Guildford from the Banks of the Wey, *oil, 1801 (Tate Gallery, London)*

Figure 38   J. M. W. Turner, A Barge on the River: Sunset, *oil, c. 1801 (Tate Gallery, London)*

In these early paintings, Turner responds to the imagery provided by a newly industrialized world with *occasional* interest in its details and effects. His painting, *A Barge on the River: Sunset* (Figure 38), has a characteristically precise title and, on the right, Turner has plainly enjoyed exploring the effect of the blazing fire. Yet this modest interest in industrial imagery is at the same time tempered by the appearance of subjects which, although they could have been treated as 'modern' pictures, Turner has painted as old-fashioned genre pictures in imitation of the old masters (something he was always trying to do). Such a painting is Figure 39, *The Blacksmith's Shop*.[1]

Figure 39   J. M. W. Turner, The Blacksmith's Shop, *oil, exhibited 1807 (Tate Gallery, London)*

Two other paintings of England from 1807 and 1815 illustrate Turner's concerns in his early period: Figure 40, *The Thames Near Walton Bridge* and Figure 41, *Crossing the Brook*. Figure 40 is like his other topographical paintings – a scene taken from his travels around England containing little yet of the poet's imagination, but with much more of a personal style. Indeed, this Turner of about 1807 looks very like a Constable of perhaps ten years later, with its aggressively painted, broad brush-strokes.

---

[1]This picture does, in fact, have an alternative title (*A Country Blacksmith Disputing upon the Price of Iron*) which has a more modern ring to it.

Figure 40 J. M. W. Turner, The Thames near Walton Bridge, *oil, 1807 (Tate Gallery, London)*

Figure 41 J. M. W. Turner, Crossing the Brook, *oil, exhibited 1815 (Tate Gallery, London)*

EXERCISE

Compare Figure 40, *The Thames Near Walton Bridge* with Figure 41, *Crossing the Brook.*

DISCUSSION

The Thames Near Walton Bridge is a topographical painting of an individual site, painted in a personal style. *Crossing the Brook,* on the other hand, is physically a much larger picture with a correspondingly enhanced presence. It is plainly an imitation of Claude. It seems that, while painters at the end of the eighteenth century began to move away from the formalized landscape of Claude towards a treatment of English topography, Turner was doing the opposite. Although *Crossing the Brook* is a painting of an English scene, (the Tamar Valley in Devon), it relies for its effect wholly on the type of visual experience made famous by Claude. As his style matured, Turner had recourse to refer to certain old masters to rival their effects. Grand pictures like this one, in which he learnt to handle a physically large canvas, prepared Turner for the 'steamy' paintings of his later career.

Figure 42   J. M. W. Turner, Rome from the Vatican, *oil, 1819–20 (Tate Gallery, London)*

Much of Turner's mature period (1820–40) was taken up with pictures derived from his experience of travel abroad. Unlike Constable, Turner travelled extensively, always in search of new experience with which to charge his paintings. These foreign paintings should not detain us here, except to make the salutary remark that Turner, despite his enormous and sustained success, was not entirely unbesmirched by ludicrous excesses. One painting produced after his first Italian trip, *Rome from the Vatican* (Figure 42), demonstrates many of Turner's weaknesses as an artist. The picture shows Raphael and his mistress, La Fornarina, selecting paintings to decorate the Vatican loggia. It is an act of piety towards Rome and to the old masters whom Turner was for ever trying to emulate. The painting shows Turner's imperfect chronology (the painting in the foreground is clearly meant to be a Claude – an anachronism), and his figure painting is as weak as his history. If Homer nods, then here Turner blinks: *Rome from the Vatican* is a poor and misguided painting.

Turner's experience of the Alps, of Italy and of the misty beauty of Venice taught him to capture the grandest of effects in his paintings. By the 1840s he was ready to interpret these effects, which nature had taught him, in more homespun but no less dramatic pictures. In his later works Turner recaptures the individual experience of the *eye,* rather in the same way as Constable recaptures the experience of the *place.* The paragon of this type of painting, where optical experience is made eternal, is *Snowstorm* (Figure 43).

In this picture Turner has captured the full effect which he experienced while he was voluntarily lashed to the mast of a steamboat during a storm off Harwich. It is a remarkable example of an artist's dedication to first-hand experience: at sixty-seven, Turner was not expected to survive the ordeal, but he did and captured the effects of turbulence, snow and a storm at sea on this canvas. If this painting suggests that Turner's pictures were *not* visionary, it is worthwhile remembering that earlier paintings like *The Slave Ship: Fire at Sea* (Figure 44), while, perhaps, being based on an actual event, were in fact products of the imagination of an artist bent on creating a picture of the sublime.

Figure 43 J. M. W. Turner, Snowstorm: Steamboat off a Harbour's Mouth, *oil, 1842 (Tate Gallery, London)*

Figure 44 J. M. W. Turner, The Slave Ship: Fire at Sea, *oil, c. 1835 (Tate Gallery, London)*

Turner was so various an artist that we can find, at one place or another in his career, an example of every separate artistic concern of the first half of the nineteenth century. You should not be surprised to find in Turner's works few illustrations of the developments of an industrializing Britain. Turner certainly had an eye for the latest detail (some of his marine pictures contain references to modern apparatus), but his art was too involved with the ideals of romanticism to be tied to any programme.

Turner, with his strong, creative imagination and his poetic imagery, is typical of the romantic artist. It was not that he turned his back on the changes to be seen around him and took refuge in an intoxicating type of art which had little social responsibility, but that his vision worked on such a grand scale that – in terms of the breadth of his experience – motifs of an industrialized society were relatively modest coals for the fuel of his fire. When he did use one of them, as we shall see below, it was in a context that can be understood best in terms of romanticism.

Turner loved power and fear: a snowstorm, an avalanche or a fire stimulated his imagination; urban poverty did not. He was in awe of the natural force of the Alps and wherever he could, he turned a scene into an expression of the sublime. Typical of this attitude is *Rain, Steam and Speed* (Figure 45). This painting was Turner's idea of how to represent the modern sublime.

Figure 45   J. M. W. Turner, Rain, Steam and Speed, *oil, 1844 (National Gallery, London)*

EXERCISE

What does *Rain, Steam and Speed* represent?

DISCUSSION

This picture, so full of dynamism and power, is a representation of a railway train passing over Brunel's bridge across the Thames between Taplow and Maidenhead. If you remember that when Turner's career began there were no railways in England, but that by the 1840s 'railway mania' was at its height, you will then begin to understand why the motif of the speeding train interested a painter of the sublime and the grand effect. Turner has made the train appear out of the steam like a terrifying beast of modern mythology, radiating power, noise and aggression. As if, in a symbol, nature is to be seen on the run from technology, Turner has also painted a frightened hare, hopelessly trying to outrun the train. At this late stage in his career, Turner had exhausted nature as a source of imagery and had made a decisive turn towards the modern world.

Rain, Steam and Speed is an insubstantial painting in that its effect is achieved by creating senses of *light* and *speed*, not tangible objects. In this it contrasts markedly with Constable's pictures, which are full of the substance of nature itself – trees, rivers and sky. This contrast is emphasized in comparing the two painters' techniques of studying nature: Constable would stare, enchanted, at a scene for long periods, slowly, meditatively absorbing its details. Turner preferred the effect of shock. Just as he was strapped to the mast to gain experience for painting the *Snowstorm*, the traditional story is that Turner learnt about the experience of the railway by leaning out of the window of a moving train. Blinded by the rain, the steam and the speed, he transferred his experience on to the canvas.

46

3.3   JOHN RUSKIN AND HISTORICISM

While Constable and Turner were painting pictures whose purpose was wholly aesthetic and exhibiting them to a distinguished public at the Royal Academy, a new attitude to art was developing in Britain and abroad, which was investing it with the power to reform society and make people good. The art of Constable and Turner was not intended to reform or to preach: it was an art for a public which wanted to buy pictures to hang on its walls; but while they were painting their masterpieces, changes in the world outside were already making this sort of art redundant. That two different types of art could coexist is remarkable enough, but that one man should provide the link between the two is even more remarkable. That man was John Ruskin.

Ruskin was, at twenty-two, the champion of Turner, rising to his defence in a book with the grandiose title, *Modern Painters: their superiority in the art of landscape painting to all The Ancient Masters, proved by examples of The True, the Beautiful and the Intellectual, from the works of modern artists, especially from those of J. M. W. Turner Esq., RA.* But Ruskin was also a moralist. His morality was not that of a Constable or a Wordsworth, who used the word in reference to a sort of pantheism, but was ethical and socio-political in origin. It was this strand of John Ruskin's thought which came to have the greatest influence on posterity. In his book *Ruskin Today* (page xii), Sir Kenneth Clark maintained that, at the first meeting of the Parliamentary Labour Party, most members owned that the major influence in their political education had been John Ruskin: the champion of Turner had come a long way. (For a taste of Ruskin's political philosophy see 'The Veins of Wealth' in your Reader, pages 262–8.)

John Ruskin had been moved to write his defence of Turner in response to a critical article in *Blackwood's Magazine,* a leading literary periodical of the time. He was moved to come to the defence of the Pre-Raphaelite Brotherhood for the same reason. When attacked, he brought his eloquence to the defence of these Victorian medievalists.

Ruskin was as various and confusing a man as Turner. His opinions are often contradictory and his titles misleading. His article 'Pre-Raphaelitism' was published in August 1851 but was, in fact, concerned largely with Turner and social

Figure 46   J. M. W. Turner, Norham Castle, Sunrise, *oil, c. 1835–40 (Tate Gallery, London)*

47

conditions. If it is at first difficult to understand how the same man could admire such different types of picture as Turner's *Norham Castle, Sunrise* (Figure 46) and Holman Hunt's *The Finding of the Saviour in the Temple* (Figure 47), it can be explained: for Ruskin admired moral truth above everything else. In the one case, he admired the truth of natural effect in Turner, and in the other, he admired the truth to an ethical cause in Holman Hunt.[1]

Figure 47   William Holman Hunt, The Finding of the Saviour in the Temple, *oil, 1854–60 (City Art Gallery, Birmingham)*

The following quotation helps:

> There is nothing that I tell you with more eager desire that you should believe . . . than this, that you never will love art well, till you love what she mirrors better.
> (*The Eagle's Nest*, Lecture III)

Ruskin's moral bludgeon intimidated art in England during the period when industrialization made its most rapid advances. (We saw that the development of the railway in Turner's lifetime produced in his art, towards the end of his life, a memorable image of this modern invention.)

It is worth recalling that, during the period when Ruskin was publishing the various volumes of *Modern Painters,* Karl Marx was working on *Das Kapital* and *The Communist Manifesto* (also in London). If industrialization can be said to have done one single thing it was to divide man from his work. Both Ruskin and Marx drew attention to the division of life between work and play since the appearance of the machine, but their solutions to the resulting problem were different, as one might expect. Ruskin glanced backwards to an imaginary medieval world where the craftsman was in love with his work: to him, handicraft offered redemption. This side of Ruskin's character (now completely different from the champion of Turner) was typical of the sentimental nostalgia common around the middle of the nineteenth century. Industrialization had jerked art out of phase with society, and cut both off from nature: the response of many thinking people was to look back at the Middle Ages with an attitude of wistful longing for a harmony that never ever really existed.

[1]Ruskin's contrariness can be emphasized by mentioning that he disliked Constable's sort of truth and was so rude about the work of Whistler (some of whose pictures look very much like Turner's) that the American artist sued him.

When this attitude appears in art it is known as 'historicism'[1] and has been the subject of many books. Historicism is a phenomenon of an unsure age, when, because of great social changes, people feel insecure and look to the past for an idea of security.[2] The novelist Sir Walter Scott, author of countless medieval romances, did much to give form to this idea and had built for himself a house in Scots Baronial style to give a dynastic gloss to his family and offspring. Other *arrivistes* also dignified themselves by the trappings of the past.

Figure 48 *East view of Abbotsford, Roxburghshire, designed for Sir Walter Scott by William Atkinson, 1816 and 1822 (National Monuments Record of Scotland, Edinburgh)*

But there was also a serious, philosophical side to historicism. As Ruskin was the moralist of painting, so Augustus Northmore Welby Pugin (1812–52), son of an *emigré* Frenchman, was the moralist of architecture. Pugin wrote a book which became well-known. It bore the imposing title of *Contrasts: or a Parallel between the Noble Edifices of the Middle Ages and the Corresponding Buildings of the Present Day, showing the Present Decay of Taste* and was published in 1836. It is the best-known example of nineteenth-century ethical historicism. To Pugin, modern society was out of harmony and could only be saved by a dual allegiance to Catholicism and Gothic architecture, the building style of the Middle Ages. *Contrasts*, a wholly visual book, worked by juxtaposing a scene from modern life (exaggerated in a Dickensian way) with an imagined version of the same scene in the Middle Ages (where beauty reigned and charity blessed all the needy, or so Pugin imagined).[3] Pugin's was an uncritical admiration for medieval life. His cause soon found supporters: the Cambridge Camden Society was founded in 1839 with the aims of promoting study of ancient church architecture and of restoring medieval ruins. The results of its efforts – that is to say high Victorian Gothic architecture – can still be seen in every great city in Britain today.

A similar, if less strident, form of historicism became the greatest influence on nineteenth-century painting after the death of Turner. If the origins of the moralizing architecture of the Gothic Revival lay in France, Pugin's paternal home, then the origins of moralizing painting in nineteenth-century England also lay abroad, in the writings and paintings of the German Romantics.

[1]'Historicism' is also, incidentally, the name given to Marxist method in the philosophy of history, although they do not mean the same.

[2]Some would say that the position is similar today, with a widespread concern for preserving old buildings.

[3]Thomas Carlyle's *Past and Present* (1843) adopted a similar conceit.

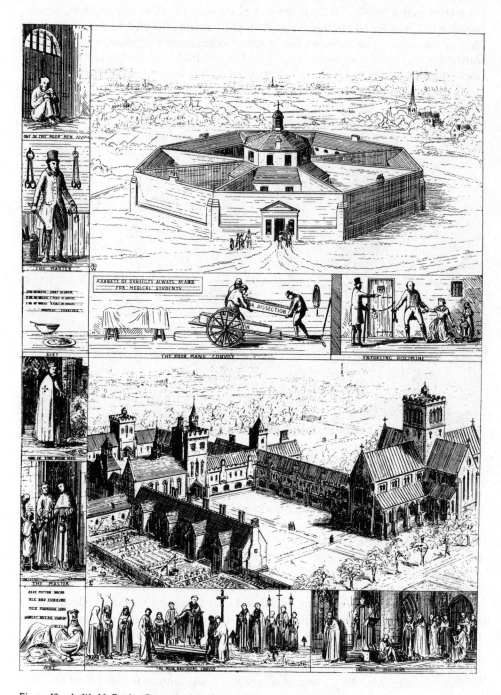

Figure 49   A. W. N. Pugin, Contrasted Residences for the Poor, 1841. *Top is the modern poor house and bottom the idealized medieval one (Photo from Pugin's* Contrasts, *reprinted in 1969 by Leicester University Press. Reproduced by kind permission of the publisher)*

4 FULL MANLY BEAUTY: THE PRE-RAPHAELITE BROTHERHOOD

4.1 ETHICS IN ART

The Pre-Raphaelite Brotherhood called itself by that extraordinary name because its intention was to take painting back to those days before Raphael (1483–1520), when it considered that art was pure, unsullied and in contact with nature. This historicism (see page 49) is an entirely modern phenomenon. During the eighteenth century the idea of progress had been a perpetual stimulus. The German romantics probably reacted consciously against the glacial, progressive, nationalist philosophy of the Enlightenment, and began to look not to the future of a well-ordered state, but to the past of mystery, fear and submission to the authority of God. In 1773 Goethe had written his encomium on the architect of the Gothic Strasbourg Cathedral and in 1791 Wilhelm Wackenroeder had written his peculiar book *Herzensergiessungen eines kunstliebenden Klosterbruder (Outpourings from the Heart of an Art-loving Monk).*[1] Goethe's was a scholarly enthusiasm, but Wackenroeder had the idea (rather as Pugin was to do) that good art could only flourish when it was in healthy relation to religion and society.

One of the single great influences on the creation of the English Pre-Raphaelite Brotherhood was the German group of artists known as the Nazarenes, who worked in a deserted monastery on the Pincian Hill in Rome. They were first known as the Saint Luke Brotherhood, after the patron saint of the guilds of medieval artists, but Peter Cornelius (1783–1867) changed their name. The Nazarenes wanted their art to be dedicated to the idea of truth to nature, uninhibited by the academic conventions of the eighteenth century; they saw this ideal at its best in the art of the high Middle Ages. Yet the clarity of their style was rather closer to that of Raphael, or, at least, Raphael's master, Perugino, than to the anonymous masters of the fifteenth century.

Figure 50 Johann Friedrich Overbeck, The Wise and Foolish Virgins, *drawing (Staatliche Graphische Sammlung, Munich)*

[1]In fact, the enthusiasm for the past was not restricted to the admirers of Gothic. Ingres, the great French classical painter, had an admiration for the fifteenth century and around the circle of Jacques-Louis David there gathered a group of artists known as 'Les Barbus' who grew beards in imitation of Homeric heroes, wore classical garb and – stoically – bathed in the ice-cold water of the wintry Seine.

What the Nazarenes saw in medieval art which they felt to be lacking in modern art was a unity of craft and art and a spirit of morally guided common purpose. This, to an extent, they achieved.

Their work became known in England because at the beginning of the nineteenth century there was something of an enthusiasm for things German. The Nazarenes were patronized by Sir Thomas Lawrence (the President of the Royal Academy who had shown such little enthusiasm for Constable's paintings) as well as by the Ecclesiological Society. Pugin, as might be expected, was an admirer, but their Catholic religiosity did not bring them any widespread popular acclaim in England. Indeed, they were something of a butt for anti-art jokes. *Punch* carried cartoons about them – Figure 51, for instance.

THE GERMAN SCHOOL.

Figure 51   The German School, *cartoon (Photo from* Punch, *Vol. X. 1846. page 145).*

During the late eighteenth and the early nineteenth centuries a taste was developed for the art of the Italian primitive. William Roscoe (whose collection of Italian paintings forms the core of that school in Liverpool's Walker Art Gallery) wrote a book on Lorenzo de' Medici;[1] Italian primitives had already been collected in the eighteenth century; Lord Lindsay wrote his *Sketches of the History of Christian Art* and in 1836 a government committee had recommended that the state buy distinguished Italian works of art. Thus it is easy to see how the Pre-Raphaelite Brotherhood might have considered the old art of Italy as a legitimate source of inspiration.[2] Starting with the primitives as a basis, and also claiming allegiance to nature as a source, the Pre-Raphaelites combined a technique of masterly realism with a new vocabulary of images to express important ethical ideas in art.

The Brotherhood was formed in 1848 with Dante Gabriel Rossetti, William Holman Hunt, John Everett Millais, William Michael Rossetti, F. G. Stephens, James Collinson and Thomas Woolner as founder members. The Brotherhood made its declaration of artistic intent at the Royal Academy in 1849 when Hunt and Millais exhibited the first two Pre-Raphaelite pictures: *Rienzi* (Figure 52) and *Lorenzo and Isabella* (Figure 53).

[1]Roscoe is very interesting besides. He was elected first president of the Liverpool Royal Institution in 1817 and delivered a speech called 'On the Origin and Vicissitudes of Literature, Science and Art, and their Influence on the Present State of Society', an account of the place of industry in the state.

[2]In actual fact it was engravings of the Campo Santo in Pisa which provided one of the major stimuli for the Brotherhood.

Figure 52 William Holman Hunt, Rienzi, oil, exhibited 1849 (Photo from the Royal Academy of Arts, London)

Figure 53 John Everett Millais, Lorenzo and Isabella, oil, exhibited 1849 (Walker Art Gallery, Liverpool)

Hunt took his subject from Bulwer-Lytton's novel, *Rienzi, Last of the Roman Tribunes*. The episode Hunt chose to depict shows, to quote the title of the painting in full, 'Rienzi vowing to obtain justice for the death of his young brother, slain in a skirmish between the Colonna and Orsini factions'. The precise details of the content need not detain us here, but the spirit of it should. In this painting Hunt wants to show elevated spirits by painting Rienzi, the freedom-loving revolutionary and liberator of Rome. It is significant that at the time Hunt was preparing for this painting (during 1848), the great year of revolutions throughout Europe, he would have been able to meet various Italian political exiles who were guests at Rossetti's house in London. In terms of the painter's style, the picture is vibrant and garishly bright, being painted from real models in the open air (in fact, in Hampstead).

Hunt's *Rienzi* was hung next to Millais's *Lorenzo and Isabella* at the Academy. Contemporary opinion welcomed what it considered to be the 'antiquarianism' of the two paintings. The *Athenaeum*, for instance, thought that Millais's canvas showed rather more *resource* than Hunt's, and that the latter was affected. The *Art Journal* thought that both were impressive as modern examples of 'old' art.

Millais, too, used a literary source for his picture: Keats's *Isabella and the Pot of Basil*. The poem runs:

> They could not in the same mansion dwell,
> Without some stir of heart, some malady.

In accordance with the principles of the Pre-Raphaelites, Millais did not paint this picture from artificial, professional, bored models, but from actual friends and acquaintances, not jaded by art but enlivened by it. Accordingly, the man at the end of the table with the glass held to his lips, is Dante Gabriel Rossetti, himself the genius of the movement.

It was characteristic of Pre-Raphaelitism that both these pictures were based on Italian subjects (even if they were interpreted by English writers). This points to one of the anomalies of the 'philosophy' of the movement. In their art the painters sought accurately to represent real models (hence the painting from life in the open air), but they often felt compelled to clothe the models in historical costume. While they wanted to moralize about the modern world, to preach with their brushes, they often got dragged back by the past. It was as if some of the social issues they were intent on depicting in their art could, for a moment, be avoided by lingering in the Middle Ages.

Figure 54   William Holman Hunt, The Awakening Conscience, *oil, Exhibited 1854 (Tate Gallery, London)*

EXERCISE

Look at Figure 54, *The Awakening Conscience*, by Holman Hunt. Can you interpret what is going on in this picture?

DISCUSSION

This is a Pre-Raphaelite painting of a modern subject. Looking at it with inno-cent eyes is a good test of how well a Pre-Raphaelite painting works. The Pre-Raphaelites intended their art to speak directly, yet much of the meaning is lost if we don't know the elaborate literary programme supporting the picture itself.

You might have thought that the painting showed a music lesson, or a family scene in comfortable Victorian England. In fact, the subject is a kept woman dallying with her lover. It was intended to shock. Her conscience has been stirred – or awakened – by a chance chord struck on the piano; her lover does not realize her changed state, and while her eyes stare intensely into space (suggest-ing that she realizes she is about to be saved), his expression continues to be one of unrepentant lechery.

You would have done very well understand that much from merely looking at the painting. For much of the picture's value as a work of art depends on its literary content, which mere observation cannot reveal. For instance, on the frame are inscribed two biblical quotations:

> As of the green leaves on a thick tree, some fall and some grow; so is the generation of flesh and blood.
> (Ecclesiastes 14, 18)

and

> Strengthen ye the feeble hands, and confirm ye the tottering knees; say ye to the faint hearted: Be ye strong, fear ye not; behold your God.
> (from Bishop Lowth's translation of Isaiah, 25, 3–4)

The music which has so affected the girl is from 'Oft in the Stilly Night', while the musical setting to Tennyson's 'Tears, Idle Tears' lies on the floor. This theme of lost souls, of redemption and of improvement, was often discussed among the members of the Pre-Raphaelite Brotherhood, and was also a characteristic of the poems of, for example, Coventry Patmore. The idea of music being the key to salvation had been suggested to Hunt by another passage from the Bible: 'As he that taketh away a garment in cold weather, so is he that singeth songs to a heavy heart'. Hunt's intention was to suggest that the idle lover, careless of the emotions of the circumstances, might be the unconscious bearer of a divine revelation, brought through the agency of music, and he included plenty of modern symbols in his picture to make sure that his audience would not miss his point. Underneath the table a cat is toying with a bird, while the design of the wallpaper follows an elaborate pattern conceived by the artist: 'the corn and vine are left unguarded by the slumbering cupid-watchers and the fruit is left to be preyed on by thievish birds'. The allegory in the picture was thus made clear.

Interestingly, Ruskin, when he was writing about the painting, remarked on what he called the 'fatal newness' of the appearance of the furniture, as if to suggest that no man who furnished his house with new (and, therefore, by 1854, factory-made) furniture could be in any way morally scrupulous. It is an interest-ing point and underlines the sentimental historicism which was the essence of Pre-Raphaelitism. Besides the religiosity and the reverence for old Italian art, two other characteristics of mid-Victorian culture can be detected in Pre-Raphaelite art:

a Historicism
In the first half of the nineteenth century, information about archaeology increased enormously. In architecture, for instance, what had before been

vaguely neo-classical became, through increasing knowledge, *Greek* Revival. Bible criticism also progressed. German scholars began critically to examine the text of the Bible and men like D. F. Strauss (who wrote *Leben Jesu* in 1835–6) applied modern historical method to a source which had not before been examined in this way. In poetry too there was an enthusiasm for the Middle Ages: in Tennyson, for instance, there is a marked community of feeling with Pre-Raphaelite art. His *Poems, Chiefly Lyrical* were published in 1830 and, although they predated the foundation of the Brotherhood, there is in them also moral comment dressed up in accurately evoked medieval disguise. In 1833 Tennyson had published 'The Lady of Shalott', a poem which was to provide ready plunder for artists intent on depicting a glamorized medieval theme. Waterhouse took advantage of this (Figure 55).

Figure 55   John William Waterhouse, The Lady of Shalott, *oil, 1888 (Tate Gallery, London)*

b   Observation

Artists and writers in the age of industrialization were fascinated by detail, both in novels and pictures. In his *Academy Notes* of 1858 John Ruskin, who became more and more interested in geology as his career progressed,[1] wrote what is now one of the *loci classici* of the love of detail. He is writing about Figure 56, John Brett *The Stonebreaker*:

> . . . It is a marvellous picture and may be examined inch by inch with delight; though nearly the last stone I should ever have thought of anyone's sitting down to paint, would have been a chalk flint. If he can make so much of that what will Mr Brett not make of mica slate and gneiss! If he can paint so lovely a distance from the Surrey downs and railway traversed vales, what would he not make of the chestnut groves of the Val d'Aosta! I heartily wish him good speed and long exile.[2]
> (John Ruskin, *Academy Notes*, page 31)

[1]There is, in the Ashmolean Museum, Oxford, a pen and ash and body colour drawing by Ruskin of a piece of rock (1853).

[2]In fact Brett exhibited a painting called *Val d'Aosta* in the Academy in 1859 but Ruskin was not enthusiastic about it, admiring the detail but deploring the lack of feeling.

Figure 56 John Brett, The Stonebreaker *oil, 1857–8 (Walker Art Gallery, Liverpool)*

Ruskin's knowledge of stones reminds us that this was the period of classification in European culture when the natural world was being observed and ordered more determinedly and more scientifically than ever before – as with Luke Howard's work on clouds, for example. Ruskin, though, did not always admire the pursuit of detail in paintings: see his comparison of Millais and Turner in your Reader, pages 313–4.

Of the Pre-Raphaelite painters it was Holman Hunt who had the most acute eye. It was said that, on one of his occasional trips to the Middle East (whither he went in pursuit of accurate backgrounds for his religious paintings), he could see, from one of the hills near Jerusalem, the satellites of Jupiter with his naked eye.

English art, even among the French, had a reputation for accurate research and for detail. The comparison of Hunt or Millais with Turner is very revealing. Once accused of 'indistinctness', Turner replied that indistinctness was his forté.

Look at Millais's *Ophelia* (Figure 57). The painting is crammed with accurately observed detail. The model was required to lie in a bath while Millais sketched,

Figure 57 John Everett Millais, Ophelia, *oil, 1851 (Tate Gallery, London)*

and when painting the flora, Millais used notes and sketches he had made along the banks of the Thames near Surbiton. There is a story[1] that a professor of botany, one day being unable to take his students on a field trip, took them to the Guildhall instead to examine Millais's *Ophelia*!

The programme of the Pre-Raphaelite Brotherhood was elaborate: it crystallized many of the strains of development which had been beneath the surface of European art throughout the century. Many years after the Brotherhood had fallen apart Percy Bate defined its aims:

> a   To have genuine ideas to express
>
> b   To study nature attentively, so as to know how to express them
>
> c   To sympathise with what is direct and serious and heartfelt in previous art, to the exclusion of what is conventional and self-parading, and learned by rote; and
>
> d   Most indispensable of all, to produce good pictures and statues.
>
> (Percy Bate, *The English Pre-Raphaelite Painters; Their Associates and Successors*, 1899, page 8)

By the mid 1850s the Brotherhood had effectively collapsed. The idea of common purpose had been abandoned for the pursuit of individual goals.

While the Brotherhood flourished it is tempting to see in the works of the Pre-Raphaelite painters a search for certainty in an unsure age, expressed in their love of detail and their taste for research. At best, these twin ends produced memorable masterpieces; at worst – where the attention to surface overwhelmed any expression of life – the results are only risible. What is certain, however, is that the Pre-Raphaelite Brotherhood and its art spawned a vast heritage which influenced the art of Britain until the end of the century.

4.2   FORD MADOX BROWN

Ford Madox Brown was not one of the original members of the Pre-Raphaelite Brotherhood, but his art made many of their principles well known.

Sir Arthur Elton (in *Art and the Industrial Revolution*) saw the Pre-Raphaelite movement as consciously attempting to evade the question of the industrial predicament. He found that by the end of the 1850s 'the few British artists still prepared to treat industrial themes . . . central to their society chose to concentrate on the simple dignity of the labourers'. John Brett's *The Stonebreaker* (Figure 56) was an example of this, although a picture of a child, and so was the slightly earlier version of the same subject by Henry Wallis (Figure 58).

When Wallis exhibited this picture at the Royal Academy in 1858 he appended to the catalogue entry a quotation from Carlyle's *Sartor Resartus* which evoked an idea of the hardship of labour:

> Hardly entreated brother! For us was thy back so bent, for us were thy straight limbs and fingers so deformed; thou wert our conscription when the lot fell, and fighting our battles wert so marred. For in thee too lay a God-created form, but it was not to be unfolded; encrusted must it stand with the thick adhesions and defacement of labour; and thy body like thy soul was not to know freedom.
> (Birmingham City Art Gallery *Catalogue*, 1960, page 149)

Wallis's attitude to the hardship of labour is interesting and compares well with contemporary representations of work in art from continental

---

[1]Most recently told in Peter Conrad's *The Victorian Treasure House*, Collins, 1973, page 109.

Figure 58   Henry Wallis, The Stonebreaker, *oil, 1857 (City Art Gallery, Birmingham)*

Europe. Because of Gustave Courbet, realism in Europe had developed a political character, and Courbet, too, had painted a picture of stonebreakers, entirely
and deliberately devoid of sentiment. But most French paintings of workmen
tended to be quaint and pastoral in substance: although Millet's *The Man with a
Hoe* (Figure 59) did show brutalized labour, in the mid-nineteenth century the
average French worker was rural rather than urban and hence susceptible to
sentimental, pastoral treatment in art. This was not the case in industrialized
England where Ford Madox Brown, like Henry Wallis, drew upon Thomas
Carlyle to lend inspiration to one of the most enduring allegorical paintings of
the last century.

Figure 59   Jean-Francois Millet, The Man with a Hoe, *oil, 1860–62 (Private collection)*

a   'Work'

Figure 60   Ford Madox Brown, Work, *oil, 1852–68 (City of Manchester Art Galleries)*

Brown's intentions in painting *Work* (Figure 60) were reformist, if not as commitedly socialist as Courbet's. Brown had admitted to socialist sympathies and in this picture he has used his art to illustrate them.

Around the frame of the painting there are four quotations from the Bible.[1] They are:

Left   Neither did we eat any man's bread for nought; but wrought with labour and travail night and day. (2 Thessolonians 3[8])

Right   Seest thou a man diligent in his business? He shall stand before Kings. (Proverbs 22[29])

Centre   I must work while it is day for night comes when no man can work. (John 9[4])

Below   In the sweat of thy face shalt thou eat bread. (Genesis 3[19])

These Biblical quotations express perfectly that curious blend of socialism and the work ethic which characterize much of high Victorian thought.

The view is of Heath Street, Hampstead on a hot July afternoon, taken halfway up the street, from the west side. Thomas Carlyle and F. D. Maurice are depicted on the right; the younger lady is Mrs Brown, the painter's wife; the man on the horse is the painter, R. B. Martineau. Brown wrote a full account of this picture which is reprinted in your Reader, pages 316–20.

One of the many purposes of Brown's painting was to elevate the British navvy so that he would become a suitable subject for art – as suitable as, in his own words, 'the peasant of the Campagna' or 'the Neapolitan *lazzarone*' had once been. One of his other aims was to dignify the working man in his 'manly health and beauty'. He also intended a reading of the painting which suggested a relative interpretation of the effort and the worth of the different navvies. One of

---

[1]The full-size version of the painting is in the Manchester City Art Gallery. There is a smaller replica in Birmingham.

them is said to be 'perhaps a trifle tough in those regions where compassion is said to reside', but the painting is nevertheless full of that righteous awe which the Victorian middle classes felt when they met or saw one of these brutes of labour at work in their genteel suburbs.

Indeed, in Brown's painting there may be detected a touch of expiated guilt by an artist of the middle classes. He wrote about the pastrycook's tray:

> For some years after returning to England[1] I could never quite get over a certain socialistic twinge on seeing it pass, unreasonable as the feeling may have been.
> (Reader, page 317)

And in the background of the picture an old lady can be seen distributing improving tracts entitled 'The Hodman's Haven; or, Drink for Thirsty Souls'. An expiation by aggrandising the role of the labourer can also be detected. Of the man with the beer tray Brown wrote, half despising, half admiring him:

> . . . A specimen of town pluck and energy contrasted with country thews and sinews. He is hump-backed, stunted in his growth, and in all matters of taste vulgar as Birmingham can make him look in the nineteenth century. As a child he was probably starved, stunted with gin and suffered to get run over. But energy has brought him through to be a prosperous beer-man and 'very much respected', and in his way a sort of hero.
> (Reader, page 318)

Ford Madox Brown's *Work* was a monumental allegory of his own philosophy, but this philosophy was strongly influenced by Carlyle. Thomas Carlyle's *Past and Present* was published in 1843, a work of high morality. In it he writes

> A man perfects himself by working. Foul jungles are cleared away, fair seed-fields rise instead, and stately cities; and withal the man himself first ceases to be a jungle and foul unwholesome desert thereby.
> (from Chapter XI, Book III of *Past and Present*. The whole text of the chapter is reprinted in your Reader, pages 241–4)

The same morality was written on to the title page of Ford Madox Hueffer's biography of Brown:

> Work! which beads the brow, and tans the flesh
> Of lusty manhood, casting out its devils!
> By whose weird art transmitting poor men's evils,
> Their bed seems down, their one dish ever fresh.
> (Ford Madox Hueffer, *Ford Madox Brown*, title page)

But, of course, life for the real labouring man was by no means as noble as Thomas Carlyle or Ford Madox Brown liked to see it.

Henry Mayhew's *London Labour and the London Poor* (1851–61) painted a different picture. One navvy Mayhew interviewed told him an elaborate story about redundancy, bad luck, injury and hardship, adding at the end:

> I went to a lodging-house in the Borough, and I sold all my things – shovel and grafting-tool and all, to have a meal of food. When all my things was gone, I didn't know where to go . . . If I could get any interest, I should like to go away as an emigrant. . . . This country is getting very bad for labour; it's so overrun with Irish that the Englishman hasn't a chance in his own land to live.
> (Henry Mayhew, *London Labour and London Poor*, vol. 3, pages 420–21)

[1]Brown was born in Calais and spent much of his youth abroad.

b 'The Last of England'

Emigration was a live issue in England in the 1850s and 1860s.[1] Many artists treated the theme.

Figure 61   Thomas Webster, A Letter from the Colonies, *oil, 1852 (Tate Gallery, London)*

Webster's painting (Figure 61) is a sentimental treatment of a family scene when a letter has been received from a departed relative; Nichols's (Figure 63) shows an Irish labourer waiting at a railway station in England while Redgrave's painting (Figure 62) is plainly influenced by Ford Madox Brown's great emigration picture (Figure 64).

Figure 62   Richard Redgrave The Emigrant's Last Sight of Home, *oil, exhibited 1859 (Roy Miles Fine Paintings Ltd, London)*

[1]There had also been a rush to emigrate in the 1820s. Some ambitious town-planning schemes were proposed in England in an attempt to stop the exodus. See Gillian Darley, *Villages of Vision*, Architectural Press, 1975, page 82.

Figure 63 Erskine Nichol, The Emigrants, *oil, 1864 (Tate Gallery, London)*

Figure 64 Ford Madox Brown, The Last of England, *oil, 1855, (City Art Gallery, Birmingham)*

Brown and his friends had been depressed about poverty (Hueffer spoke of him 'steeping himself in Carlyle and gloom'). When things got too bad for artists Thomas Woolner, one of the founding members of the Pre-Raphaelite Brotherhood and a friend of Brown's, decided to go to Australia to join the gold rush in the hope of amassing enough money to carry on with his art. Brown accompanied Woolner and his wife as far as Gravesend and the experience gave him the idea for this painting. He even wrote a sonnet for the occasion:

> The last of England! O'er the sea, my dear,
> Our homes to seek amid Australian fields.
> Us, not our million-acred island yields
> The space to dwell in. Thrust out. Forced to hear
> Low ribaldry from sots and share rough cheer
> From rudely nurtured men. The hope youth builds
> Of fair renown, bartered for that which shields
> Only the back, and half-formed lands that rear.
>
> The dust-storm blistering up the grasses wild.
> There learning skills not, nor the poets dream,
> Nor aught so loved as children shall we see.
> She grips his listless hand and clasps her child.
> Through rainbow tears she sees a sunnier gleam.
> She cannot see a void, where he will be.
> (Robin Ironside, *Pre-Raphaelite Painters*, page 24)

It will be appreciated that Brown was not a good poet, but his painting *The Last of England* was the first of his works to attract any real praise.

To describe what is going on in the picture one can do no better than use Brown's own words, written for the catalogue of the 1865 Piccadilly Exhibition:

> The picture is, in the strictest sense, historical. It treats of the great emigration movement, which attained its culminating point in 1852. The educated are bound to their country by closer ties than the illiterate, whose chief consideration is food, and physical comfort. I have, therefore, in order to present the parting scene in its fullest tragic development, singled out a couple from the middle classes[1], high enough, through educational refinement, to appreciate all they are now giving up and yet dignified enough in means to have to put up with discomforts and humiliations incident to a vessel 'all one class'. The husband broods bitterly over blighted hopes, and severance from all he has been striving for. The young wife's grief is a less cantankerous sort, probably confined to the sorrow of parting with a few friends of early years. The circle of her love moves with her.
>
> The husband is shielding his wife from the sea-spray with an umbrella. Next to them, in the background, an honest family of the greengrocer kind, father (mother lost), eldest daughter and younger children, make the best of things with tobacco-pipe and apples, etc. etc. Still further back, a reprobate shakes his fist with curses at the land of his birth, as though that were answerable for his want of success; his old mother reproves him for his foul-mouthed profanity, while a boon companion, with flushed countenance, and got-up in nautical togs for the voyage, signifies drunken approbation. The cabbages slung round the stern of the vessel indicate, to the practised eye, a lengthy voyage; but for this their introduction would be objectless. A cabin-boy, too used to 'leaving his native land' to see occasion for much sentiment in it, is selecting vegetables for the dinner out of a boatful.
>
> . . .To insure the peculiar look of *light all round* which objects have on a dull day at sea, it was painted for the most part in the open air on dull days, and, when the flesh was being painted, on cold days. Absolutely without regard to the art of any period or country, I have tried to render this scene as it would appear. The minuteness of detail which would be visible under such conditions of broad daylight I have thought necessary to imitate as bringing the pathos of the subject home to the beholder.
> (Text reproduced in Birmingham City Art Gallery *Catalogue*, 1960, page 18)

[1]The subject is actually a self-portrait of Brown with his wife and child.

EXERCISE

What different attitudes, social and artistic, do you detect in this statement?

DISCUSSION

You would have done well to have noted, but not necessarily in this order:

1   An acute awareness of the difference between classes (as there was in his description of *Work*). It is suggested that the middle classes, by virtue of their education, are more sensitive than, say, greengrocers.

2   A frustration at prevailing conditions in England, but with the attendant feeling that the country must not be blamed as the reprobate blames it.

3   The use of symbolism.

4   A strict attention to painterly detail. The text suggests that the models were painted in conditions designed to simulate the discomforts of the voyage.

5   A lack of regard for any artistic precedent. In Brown's view this was an entirely 'modern' picture.

6   The condescending attitude to woman. Brown suggests that the emigrant's thoughts on his departure are bound to be on a higher plane than those of his wife.

7   Moral condemnation of the drunken reprobate together with a highly sentimentalized view of the mother figure.

If Brown thought that his *Last of England* was a modern picture he was right, because its concern with a modern social issue and its elaborate artistic programme were to become characteristic features of later nineteenth-century British art.

Figures 65a (top), 65b (middle), 65c (bottom) August Egg, Past and Present Nos 1, 2 and 3, oil, 1858 (Tate Gallery, London). Hung as a triptych with figure 65b on the left, figure 65a in the middle and figure 65c on the right.

In his series of three paintings exhibited at the Royal Academy in 1858 (Figures 65a, b and c) Augustus Egg found an artistic use for the memorable title of *Past and Present*, Carlyle's great work of 1843. Unlike Carlyle, Egg did not want to show the decline of civilization, but, instead, a personal decline. His *Past and Present* is like a female *Rake's Progress*: a lover found out, children orphaned, the loose woman left shivering under a railway arch at Charing Cross, with everything around her a symbolic reminder of her mortal folly. It is by now a familiar story, but its treatment in art[1] was novel, for the taste for contemporary social subject-matter was, in 1860, still an unusual one. But this taste was developing. A character in Charles Kingsley's *Alton Locke* says that 'true poetry, like true charity . . . begins at home'. Just as Kingsley did not wish to avoid the day-to-day domestic tragedies of industrial life, neither did the artists. Kingsley's character goes on to say 'Just gang after your nose, and keep your eyes open and ye'll no miss it'.

That is what artists did – and the exploding cities, particularly London, gave them a treasure trove of subject matter. In Dickens there is always the idea that the city is evil and this feeling was reflected in art. When the French draughtsman, Gustave Doré, engraved plates for Blanchard Jerrold's *London: a Pilgrimage* (1872) he captured an aspect of the metropolitan scene forever and charged it fully with a sense of the unwholesome and the unhealthy.

Figure 66   Gustave Doré, Lambeth Gas Works, *engraving (Photo from Gustave Doré and Blanchard Jerrold, 1872,* London: a Pilgrimage; *reprinted in 1970 by Dover Publications. Reproduced by permission of the publisher)*

[1]Like Rossetti's *Found*, which dealt with a similar subject.

It will come as no surprise to learn that Doré, the creator of this singular image, was an admirer of that other painter who had sensed evil in the city, John Martin.

It happened that this moralizing imperative among artists occurred at about the same time as mass-circulation illustrated periodicals were really beginning to make an impression.[1] The massive demand for these illustrated papers gave employment to many artists and, perhaps for the first time, created a generalized mass culture of pictorial imagery. By the mid 1870s *The Graphic* and *The Illustrated London News* were enjoying immense fame. Thomas Hardy even recommended study of their plates as a suitable introduction to art education for children. Ruskin, too, took notice. In his *Academy Notes* of 1875 he made an interesting comment on the decline of that Salon of English High Art, the Royal Academy. Overtaken on the one side by photographers, on the other by popular illustrators,

> . . . the Royal Academy of England, in its annual publication is now nothing more than a huge coloured *Illustrated Times* folded in saloons, – the spendidest May number of *The Graphic*, shall we call it? That is to say, it is a certain quantity of pleasant, but imperfect, 'illustration' of passing events, mixed with as much gossip of the past, and tattle of the future, as may be probably agreeable to a populace supremely ignorant of the one, and reckless of the other.
> (John Ruskin, *Academy Notes*, 1875)

So, in Ruskin's view, the Academy in 1875 was no more than a coloured edition of an illustrated newspaper. How times had changed! Three men made this remarkable state of events possible: Samuel Luke Fildes (1844–1927), Hubert von Herkomer (1849–1914) and Frank Holl (1845–88). Each was connected with either, or both, *The Graphic* and *The Illustrated London News* and each made a major contribution to the character of popular imagery at the end of the century.

Figure 67   Luke Fildes, Homeless and Hungry, *engraving, from* The Graphic, *4 December 1874 (Mary Evans Picture Library)*

Fildes had helped to launch *The Graphic* when it first appeared in 1869. The original illustrator of Dickens's *Edwin Drood*, Fildes was first to create in England that style-label we know as 'social realism'. Like the character in *Alton Locke*, Fildes went out 'after his nose' and painted the scenes of misery and deprivation which any circuit of an industrial city in the 1870s would produce. His *Homeless and Hungry* (Figure 67) appeared in the first edition of *The Graphic* and was later worked up into a full-scale painting with a different title, *Applicants for Admission to a Casual Ward* (Figure 68).

---

[1]*Punch* founded 1841, *The Illustrated London News* founded 1842, *The Graphic* founded 1869, *The Pictorial Times* founded 1843.

Figure 68 Luke Fildes, Applicants for Admission to a Casual Ward, *oil, 1874 (Collection, Royal Hollo-way College, University of London)*

As if the brutal shock of this sort of social reporting in art was too much to sustain indefinitely, Fildes slipped back later in his career to a comfortable, uncritical historicism which lacked any edge. At a wedding in Oxfordshire in the 1880s he complained of having to paint tawdry shop goods and in *An Alfresco Toilette* (Figure 69) he reveals the late-Victorian idea that to paint with masterly virtuosity, in hot pursuit of nature, absolved the artist from having to do anything else at all.

Figure 69 Luke Fildes, An Alfresco Toilette, *oil, 1889 (The Lady Lever Art Gallery, Port Sunlight)*

Figure 70   Hubert von Herkomer, Hard Times, *oil, 1885 (City of Manchester Art Galleries)*

As well as being a painter of some talent, the immigrant Hubert von Herkomer (1849–1914) was a mesmerist, musician, writer, film-maker and dramatist. He also succeeded Ruskin as Slade Professor of Fine Art at Oxford University. Herkomer's *Hard Times* (Figure 70) tells us a lot about the state of art in the 1880s. It is an accurately depicted scene (we happen to know that it is Coldharbour Lane in Bushey, Hertfordshire)[1] and we also know that in it Herkomer intended to publicize the distress then being felt among the working classes in a late Victorian recession. Using these serious, earnest sentiments in a similar way was Frank Holl (1845–88). *At a Railway Station* (Figure 71) was typical of the type of picture which brought to the British public an awareness of the power of art as well as a clear understanding of hardship.

Figure 71   Frank Holl, At A Railway Station, *engraving, from* The Graphic, *10 February 1872*

[1]This later became known, after the painting, as Hard Times Lane.

This brief discussion of these artists who created popular illustrations would merely be diverting were it not for an important fact. Certainly, Fildes, Herkomer and Holl were almost alone in having created a still fresh (if harrowing) purpose for art in the late Victorian era. Yet it was these very works which wielded a mighty influence over Vincent Van Gogh, (a painter who also used peasants and workers as his subjects), and, therefore, over the course of development of modern European art.

Figure 72   Josef Israels, Alone in the World, *oil (Stitching Bevordering Belangen Rijksmuseum, Amsterdam)*

Van Gogh could turn to the work of his own countrymen, like Josef Israels (Figure 72), when he sought a profound expression of pessimism, or to paintings by Constantin Meunier when he wanted to know how to paint miners (Figure 73).

Figure 73   Constantin Meunier, Miners on the way Home, *oil (Copyright ACL Bruxelles, Belgium)*

Meunier's art represents a stage just about one remove away from Van Gogh's own paintings of working folk (Figure 74), but Van Gogh really took his inspiration from the English illustrators. He transformed their concern for expression of melancholy and of social injustice into his own highly individual art.

Figure 74   Vincent van Gogh, Miner with a Shovel on his Shoulder, *pen and pencil, 1879 (Rijksmuseum Kroller-Muller, Otterlo)*

So the cycle of representing the worker in art has been completed. At the beginning of our period, workers appeared in paintings as actors on a picturesque stage, while by the end of the century Vincent Van Gogh, under the influence of English illustrators, was using workers as subjects in his art of social responsibility. Even if the styles of the illustrators of *The Graphic* did not affect Van Gogh's painting, their awareness of contemporary problems did. Herkomer, Holl and Fildes were firmly established in the tradition of English art and it seems that this same tradition influenced Van Gogh, one of the major figures in the origins of modern continental art.

Yet there is an anomaly: the Pre-Raphaelite Brotherhood could be said (as they would certainly have wished) to be bringing art nearer to the people by communicating more directly. But their efforts (if you follow the development through Ford Madox Brown and *The Graphic* through to the avant-garde art of Van Gogh) did not achieve that end. Indeed, it is an appropriate footnote to the age which produced Marx's economic theory, that the process which tended to estrange art from society was begun at that time.

GLOSSARY

ACADEMY   The London Royal Academy, which was founded in 1768, later than the Academies of Italy and France. It was essentially a society of artists. The word 'academic' has now come to mean traditional and conservative.

AQUATINT   see ENGRAVING

BEDLAM   A contraction of *Bethlehem*, after the priory of St Mary of Bethlehem which became a lunatic asylum in 1377. Later the hospital moved and became one of the famous sights of London.

BODYCOLOUR   see WATERCOLOUR.

BULWER-LYTTON   Edward George Earle Lytton, first Baron Lytton of Knebworth, English novelist, poet, playwright and politician (1803–73).

CAMPAGNA   The Italian word for countryside.

CLASSICAL   Properly of ancient Greece in its period of greatest flowering (fifth century BC), but also used to signify that which is in the tradition of Greece, Rome and Italy.

COLERIDGE   Samuel Taylor Coleridge, English poet and philosopher (1772–1834).

COURBET   Gustave Courbet, French painter (1819–77).

CRABBE   George Crabbe, English poet (1754–1832) who specialized in realistic poems of country life.

DANTE   Dante Alighieri, Italian poet (1265–1321). The author of *Vita Nuova* and *Divina Commedia*.

DAVID   Jacques-Louis David, French neoclassical painter (1748–1825).

DORE   Gustave Doré, French graphic artist (1832–82).

ECCLESIOLOGISTS   The name given to the Cambridge Camden Society and its like, whose intention was, as one such society said at the time, 'to spread . . . a just appreciation of Ecclesiastical design'.

ENCLOSURE   The Board of Agriculture was set up in 1793. Enclosure acts of the first half of the nineteenth century did to yeomen farmers what industry had done to artisans: it converted them from independent freeholders into landless labourers working for a wage.

ENGRAVING   One of the methods of reproducing prints. In engraving the lines are cut into a metal plate which is then inked. Other methods of reproduction are ETCHING (in which a metal plate is covered with a wax which is then scratched away; the plate is then immersed in acid; the wax is afterwards dissolved and the lines of the drawing carry ink where the acid has eaten into them); MEZZOTINT (where a metal plate has its surface roughened and the parts which are meant to show light in the finished print are then scraped away to reveal smooth metal) and AQUATINT (the method is similar to that of etching, but, like mezzotint, it relies on tone and not on line for its effect; each plate goes through a number of different phases of immersion in the acid to give different degrees of tone).

ETCHING   see ENGRAVING.

GOETHE   Johann Wolfgang von Goethe, German poet, playwright, novelist, scientist and statesman (1749–1832).

HAZLITT   William Hazlitt, English critic (1778–1830).

HOMER   Greek epic poet, the author of *The Iliad* and *The Odyssey* (probably eighth century BC).

INGRES   Jean August Dominique Ingres, French painter (1780–1867).

KINGSLEY   Charles Kingsley, English novelist and historian (1819–75).

LANDSCAPE   A tract of land, used usually as a tract of land perceived pictorially. From the Dutch *landskip*.

LINNAEUS   Swedish botanist (1707–78) who classified animals, vegetables and minerals.

MACPHERSON   James Macpherson, Scottish poet (1736–96) the author of a famous fraud, *The Works of Ossian* (1765) which purported to be translations of a cycle of ancient Gaelic poetry. It was highly influential and popular in the romantic era.

MEZZOTINT   see ENGRAVING.

MILLET   Jean-François Millet, French painter (1814–75).

MILTON   John Milton, English epic poet (1608–74), famous for his *Paradise Lost* (1667).

PANTHEISM   A vague word of no precise meaning, but suggestive of that attitude to the world and creation which sees life in all things and God everywhere.

PASTORAL   Properly, that which pertains to shepherds, but used to denote a mode in painting or poetry which is devoted to the countryside's idyllic character.

PATMORE   Coventry Patmore, English poet (1823–96). A friend of Rossetti and Ruskin.

POPE   Alexander Pope, English poet (1688–1744).

RAPHAEL   Raffaello Sanzio, Italian painter (1483–1520). Famous for the purity and elegance of his style.

REMBRANDT   Rembrandt Harmenszoon van Ryn, Dutch painter (1606–99).

ROMANTICISM   Romanticism has long evaded definition. One of its chief critics, F. L. Lucas, said that it was easier to detect than to define. Goethe said that it was disease, compared to classicism which was health. Essentially the romantic movement began in Germany in the later eighteenth century and spread to England and France. Mystery, fear and fascination with age and fancy were characteristics of romantic writing.

SUBLIME   From the Latin which means lofty, or elevated. Used by the English philosopher Edmund Burke in his *A Philosophical Enquiry* (1759) as the opposite to the beautiful: the sublime was that which induced a delicious sense of fear in the spectator.

TITIAN   Tiziano Vecelli, Italian painter (*c.* 1490–1576).

TOPOGRAPHY   The study of particular localities.

WASH   see WATERCOLOUR.

WATERCOLOUR   Watercolour is primarily an English medium. In it, transparent washes of paint are applied to wet paper in washes, usually leaving the white of the paper to show up as highlights. BODYCOLOUR is watercolour mixed with white so that it is no longer transparent.

RECOMMENDED READING

If you want to find out more about any of the painters mentioned in these units, Peter and Linda Murray's *Dictionary of Art and Artists* (an A101 Set Book) will provide you with useful information.

For more detailed discussion of material used in the text there are the following books which should be available in most good libraries:

Luke Herrmann (1973) *Landscape Painting in Britain in the Eighteenth Century*, Faber. An indispensable work to anyone studying the history of English landscape art. It is to be followed by a volume on the nineteenth-century landscape.

William Feaver (1975) *John Martin*, Oxford University Press. An interesting study which pays a lot of attention to Martin's literary sources.

Graham Reynolds, *Constable: the Natural Painter*. Still perhaps the best book on Constable.

Ernst Gombrich (1960) *Art and Illusion*, Pantheon Books, New York. A work of genius. It only occasionally touches upon matters related to these units, but the breadth of its understanding of crucial issues in the history of art must make it highly recommended.

A. Finberg (second edition 1961) *J. M. W. Turner, R.A.* Oxford University Press. This is the most thorough book about Turner, and because of its bulk it has attained the status of the 'standard' work, but it is by no means wholly acceptable. In fact, there is no single book on Turner which can be recommended without reservations: John Gage's *Colour in Turner* (1968), Studio Vista, is fascinating, but confusing and difficult while Luke Herrmann's *Turner* (1975), Phaidon, is largely pictorial.

Francis D. Klingender (1968) *Art and the Industrial Revolution*, revised edition by Sir Arthur Elton, Adams & Dart, Bath. A brilliant book, full of unexpected connections and novel thoughts but, you should be warned, one that uses its evidence very selectively.

BIBLIOGRAPHY

Bachelor, Thomas (1804) *Village Scenes, The Progress of Agriculture and Other Poems*, Vernor and Hood.

Bate, Percy (1899) *The English Pre-Raphaelite Painters; Their Associates and Successors*.

Beckett, R. B. (1970) *John Constable's Discourses*, Suffolk Records Society, Volume 14.

Birmingham City Art Gallery (1960) *Catalogue*.

Bloomfield, Robert (1826) *Wildflowers; or Pastoral and Local Poetry*, London.

Clark, Lord Kenneth (1967) *Ruskin Today*, Penguin.

Constable (1976) Exhibition Catalogue, Tate Gallery.

Davies, Martin (second edition 1959) *The British School*, National Gallery Catalogue.

Elton, Sir Arthur (1968) *Art and the Industrial Revolution*, Exhibition Catalogue, City Art Gallery, Manchester.

Falk, Bernard (1938) *Turner, the Painter: His Hidden Life*, Heinemann.

Ford Madox Hueffer (1896) *Ford Madox Brown*.

Gilpin, William (1786) *Observations, Relative Chiefly to Picturesque Beauty:* London.

Ironside, Robin (1948) *Pre-Raphaelite Painters*, Phaidon.

Klingender, Francis D. (revised edition 1948) *Art and the Industrial Revolution* Adams and Dart, Bath.

Mayhew, Henry (1851–61) *London Labour and London Poor*, Volume 3.

Moir, Elspeth (1964) *The Discovery of Britain*, Routledge and Kegan Paul.

Pendered, Mary (1923) *John Martin, Painter, His Life and Times*, London.

Thornbury, Walter (second edition 1877) *The Life of J. M. W. Turner R.A.*, Chatto and Windus.

A101 AN ARTS FOUNDATION COURSE

ARTS AND SOCIETY IN AN AGE OF INDUSTRIALIZATION